C000098678

TOWN & COUNTRY
BIRDS

© AA Media Limited 2011
Written by Andy Clements

Produced for AA Publishing by D & N Publishing, Baydon, Wiltshire

Commissioning editor at AA Publishing: Paul Mitchell
Production at AA Publishing: Rachel Davis

Printed and bound in China by C&C Offset Printing Co. Ltd

A CIP catalogue record for this book is available from the British
Library.

ISBN 978 0 7495 68306
      978 0 7495 68498 (SS)

Published by AA Publishing, a trading name of AA Media Limited,
whose registered office is Fanum House, Basing View, Basingstoke,
Hampshire RG21 4EA. Registered number 06112600.

A04089
theAA.com/shop

CONTENTS

INTRODUCTION

Birds are the most popular and accessible group of our wildlife, and we all come across them in everyday life. They tend to be conspicuous, many are colourful, and as there is not an overwhelming number of species in our region it is easy to get to know and understand them. In addition, their mastery of the air remains a source of wonder to humans.

This book covers the 91 species of bird most likely to be seen in England, Scotland and Wales during our day-to-day urban and rural lives. Most are common and widespread, and include such favourites as the Mallard, Woodpigeon, Robin and Blackbird. Some species with a very restricted range are included, such as the Crested Tit and Cirl Bunting, while others may have particular habitat requirements and be harder to find, such as the Hawfinch and Nightingale. The spectacular and special Red Kite, Waxwing and Firecrest are included to encourage the novice birdwatcher.

Each species is given two pages, with concise text to fit in as much information as possible. Each species account begins with the common

The ROBIN's song is one of the most familiar sounds in the garden and can be heard at most times of the year.

English name followed by the species' scientific name. The subsequent text is divided into sections: **FACT FILE**, which covers the species' size (wingspan is given only for species where flight identification is commonly required), habitat preferences, food and voice; **IDENTIFICATION**, which describes its appearance; **STATUS AND HABITS**, which describes where the species occurs, its population status, and behavioural traits that assist with identification; and **KEY FACT**, which provides tips on unique information that separates this species from close relatives. Two photographs accompany the text for each species.

Many birds of town and country are easy to find, as they live alongside people, be it in our gardens, along roadsides, or even among town and city buildings. Feral Pigeons are abundant in city centres, Song Thrushes are commoner songsters in towns nowadays than in the countryside; our village houses are home to Swifts in summer, and Kestrels are conspicuous roadside hunters seen regularly during our motorway journeys. If you feed birds in your garden, you will be able to attract a dazzling array of species by supplying a broad variety of high-quality food. Alongside the common Greenfinch, Great Tit and Blackbird, you may bring in the pretty Goldfinch, the impressive Great Spotted Woodpecker and the diminutive Siskin.

To see a wider diversity of species, visit woodland, farmland, marsh and coastal areas. Listening to the Nightingale's beautiful song on a warm summer's evening in a southern English woodland is a delight, and at dusk the characteristic hooting of a Tawny Owl may attract attention. Whitethroats are perky summer visitors, enlivening farmland hedgerows with their noticeable song flights, while in winter the same fields of stubble provide a home for Corn Buntings, and for Redwings and Fieldfares – our 'winter thrushes'. Curlew and Golden Plover flocks can be spotted on coastal mudflats in autumn and winter, while marshes in summer provide habitat for the Grey Heron and food for the Hobby – a spectacular aerial falcon capable of catching dragonflies over open water. Discover excitement in every habitat and at all times of year.

It is easy to make your birdwatching purposeful, and for your sightings to help the conservation of birds and other wildlife. The British Trust for Ornithology (www.bto.org) organises a range of surveys that rely on volunteers submitting records of the birds they have seen. You can take part in a survey of the birds that visit your garden, breeding birds of the wider countryside, and winter waterfowl of our coasts and lakes. The organisation has an online facility, called BirdTrack, that allows you to keep and access your observations while contributing data at a local, national and even international level. Conservation also relies on observers taking care not to interfere with breeding birds, and allowing flocks of winter visitors to get on with the business of feeding, preening and loafing without disturbance.

Birds are a group of vertebrates that are distinguished by having feathers, and that are generally able to fly. All British birds exercise the power of flight to some extent, although there are some birds around the globe – such as kiwis in New Zealand and the Ostrich in Africa – that have evolved a flightless lifestyle. The size and colour of different feather groups (called tracts) on a bird enable us to identify different species; examples of this are shown on the topography diagram below.

After mating, female birds lay eggs in a nest, which can be an open construction of varied size and complexity, or a hole in a tree or building. The eggs are then incubated by either or both parents until the chicks hatch. Chicks of small birds and birds of prey tend to be fairly helpless and nestbound, entirely dependent on their parents for the first few days of life. In contrast, waterfowl chicks are often running around within a day of hatching and are taught by their parents how to find food.

Many birds are migratory, some travelling huge distances across the globe. Species that spend the northern temperate summer in Britain arrive from the warmer tropics to the south and return there before the onset of our winter. Our resident winter bird populations, meanwhile, are enhanced by the arrival of other species from further north.

HOUSE SPARROW

crown
nape
mantle
throat
scapulars
wing-bar
tertials
breast
primaries
flank
rump
belly
tail
undertail coverts

Breckland Open grass heaths of East Anglia.

Covey Small group of gamebirds.

Crepuscular Active at dawn and dusk.

Cryptic Camouflaged.

Eclipse Moulted plumage of ducks in summer, which for a short period renders them flightless; eclipse males resemble females.

Facial disc Flat and usually round plumage delineating the face of an owl.

Hybridisation Interbreeding of two different species.

Incubation Sitting on eggs to keep them warm in the period up to hatching.

Invertebrates All animals that lack a backbone, including insects.

Irruptive Bird populations that suddenly move in large numbers following an abundant food supply.

Loafing When larger birds rest in flocks.

Lores Plumage between the bill and eye.

Migration Mass regular movement of bird populations from one geographical region to another.

Morph Different colour varieties of the same species.

Parasitise To use the resources of another species, such as when Cuckoos lay their eggs in the nest of another bird so that it raises their young.

Preening Care of the feathers, usually by passing feather edges through the bill.

Primaries Strong, long flight feathers occupying the outer third and tip of the wing.

Speculum Colourful band near the rear edge of a duck's wing.

Supercilium Eyebrow, often forming a clear, pale stripe on the side of the head.

Tract Group of similar feathers forming a discrete part of the plumage.

MALLARD
Anas platyrhynchos

FACT FILE

SIZE Length 50–65cm **HABITAT** Freshwater and coastal wetlands **FOOD** Mainly aquatic and land plants, some insects, small aquatic animals **VOICE** Familiar quack, given only by female; drake weakly nasal

IDENTIFICATION

Male has a glossy green head, separated from chestnut breast by narrow white collar. Body grey-brown with black stern and white tail. Bill yellow. Female has uniform brown streaked plumage and a dull orange bill. In summer, male moults into eclipse plumage, resembling female but with richer brown on breast. In flight, both sexes show a dark blue speculum, narrowly bordered white.

KEY FACT In spring, a number of drakes may all pursue one female in a noisy mêlée. This can appear to be persecution, but is usually part of complex breeding displays.

MALE

LOCATION	DATE/TIME

STATUS AND HABITS

Probably the most familiar wildfowl species in Britain. Often encountered in urban parks and around village ponds, where it can be tame and easily fed by humans. Also found amongst flocks of domestic breeds of duck. Rests and feeds in small flocks outside the breeding season, sometimes on the sea. When feeding in fresh water, it will characteristically upend. Its flight is swift and strong, pairs often twisting and turning close together, when plumage differences are obvious.

FEMALE

GREY HERON
Ardea cinerea

SIZE **Length 90–98cm** HABITAT **Wetlands,**
sometimes on coasts FOOD **Mainly fish, plus Water Voles,**
amphibians, young birds, invertebrates VOICE **Loud, harsh** *frarnk*

FACT FILE

IDENTIFICATION
Large bird with a long
yellow bill and legs, and
grey, white and black
plumage that is
distinctive at rest and
in flight. Head, neck
and underparts are
white. Black head
feathering is striped
down front and back of
neck. Huge in flight,
with bowed, rounded,
pale grey and blackish
wings; wingbeats slow;
head and neck kinked
and drawn in,
outstretched on
landing; and with long
legs trailing behind.

KEY FACT One of our earliest breeding birds, with colonies
occupied from Feb. Nests (usually in the tops of tall trees) are used year
after year, becoming very large accumulations of branches and sticks.

LOCATION	DATE/TIME

STATUS AND HABITS

The most often encountered huge bird of Britain, frequently seen standing 'priest-like' in marshland or on a winter shore. It can remain motionless for hours, either resting or waiting for prey, which it sometimes stalks in slow, deliberate strides before unleashing a lightning-fast strike. Fish are skewered and then swallowed head  first. Roosts in trees, on low rocks or on rocky islets. Crepuscular, being especially active around dawn and dusk.

BUZZARD
Buteo buteo

FACT FILE

SIZE Length 50–55cm; wingspan 115–130cm
HABITAT Mixed woodland, farmland landscapes, open hilly country
FOOD Small mammals and carrion, plus insects and earthworms in winter VOICE Mewing *peeioo*

IDENTIFICATION

Medium-sized bird of prey with rounded wings held in a shallow 'V' when soaring, and a shortish, rounded tail. Plumage is highly variable, predominantly shades of brown with paler undersides to wings and tail. Underparts are barred and streaked, with dark trailing edge to underwing. Upperparts are usually dark brown, occasionally with rufous tones. Legs and black-tipped bill are yellow.

STATUS AND HABITS

One of our commonest birds of prey, the Buzzard is found in hilly, uncultivated land in W Britain and, increasingly, above farm woodland in lowland E England. Buzzards spend long periods perched in the open on fenceposts and dead branches, and are a common sight along roadsides. They can soar for hours on end, hardly flapping their wings, and after rising on a thermal, they glide down to the next one, migrating huge distances in this way.

LOCATION	DATE/TIME

KEY FACT

The Buzzard is undergoing a rapid extension of its range across England from traditional strongholds in the W, probably enabled by reductions in persecution and less persistent chemical pollution.

RED KITE
Milvus milvus

SIZE **Length 60–65cm; wingspan 155–185cm**
HABITAT **Gently rolling wooded valleys adjacent to farmland
and open country** FOOD **Small mammals, birds, carrion and
invertebrates** VOICE **Tremulous, shrill** *weoo weoo*

IDENTIFICATION

Rangy bird of prey with reddish-brown plumage, a paler head and a long, markedly forked tail. In flight, shows paler shoulders and whitish patches to black-tipped primaries. Uppertail is rich reddish brown, underside paler. Seen from below, body and leading edge of wings are streaked reddish. Flight is buoyant, with wings kinked and tail constantly adjusting the bird's direction and height.

STATUS AND HABITS

Previously restricted to a small population in W Wales, this bird is now common and widespread thanks to recent reintroductions across Britain. Most often seen in flight (when immensely graceful and entertaining), Red Kites can now be encountered in and around towns in the Thames Valley and NE England. A social bird, it breeds in loose aggregations in broadleaved woods and gathers in winter in sizeable flocks.

LOCATION	DATE/TIME

KEY FACT

A few farms provide artificial winter feeding, where flocks gather and put on a breathtaking aerial display as birds swoop down to pick food from the ground in flight.

SPARROWHAWK
Accipiter nisus

SIZE Length 30–40cm **HABITAT** Mixed woodland, farmland and, increasingly, urban parks and gardens
FOOD Mainly small songbirds, plus some mice and insects
VOICE Harsh *kek-kek-kek*

IDENTIFICATION

Round-winged, long-tailed, medium-sized bird of prey. Male is blue-grey above with barred reddish-orange underparts, prominent white undertail feathers and a barred tail. Female is greyish brown above with whitish underparts. Juvenile is similar to a brownish female. All have barred underwings when seen in flight. Legs and black-tipped bill are yellow, and eyes are prominent yellow or orange.

MALE

LOCATION	DATE/TIME

KEY FACT

Although Sparrowhawks are often seen taking garden bird table visitors, research has shown that they are not reducing songbird populations. In fact, they have also been undergoing a recent decline.

STATUS AND HABITS

Now common and widespread, the Sparrowhawk has recovered from low numbers 50 years ago, which were the result of agrochemical pollution and persecution. Probably the commonest bird of prey seen in our towns. Its usual flight is a characteristic series of flaps and glides, often accompanied by parties of mobbing songbirds. Also soars high in the sky, and its breeding display above woodland includes spectacular dives and climbs. Hunts from ground level, with a dashing flight that surprises feeding flocks of small birds.

JUVENILE

HOBBY
Falco subbuteo

SIZE Length 28–35cm **HABITAT** Woodland edges, parkland, heathland, marshland **FOOD** Large insects (dragonflies), birds, bats **VOICE** Repeated, scolding *kew, kew, kew, kew*

FACT FILE

IDENTIFICATION

Has a black head and moustache, contrasting with white cheeks and throat, visible in both flying and perching birds. In flight, wings appear long and pointed with a short tail, recalling a large Swift. Heavily streaked and barred underparts look dark, and the red 'trousers' are surprisingly hard to see. Young birds are browner than adults, and have pale feather edgings, a pale crown and no red 'trousers'.

KEY FACT Hobbies are impressively fast and manoeuvrable flyers, able to chase down martins and Swallows. A late-summer evening visit to a Swallow roost in a marshland reedbed can provide an exciting spectacle.

LOCATION	DATE/TIME

STATUS AND HABITS

A summer visitor to Britain, generally arriving in late Apr and May. Newly arrived migrants sometimes form flocks over favoured marshes and heaths, feeding on dragonflies caught on the wing. The prey is then deftly held in the talons, dismembered and transferred to the beak, all while the bird is still flying. Breeding birds are secretive, despite nests being situated in tall trees. When the young first fly they accompany adults in hunting, their noisy calls making the birds conspicuous.

KESTREL
Falco tinnunculus

SIZE Length 30–39cm HABITAT Cultivated
landscapes, heathland, roadsides FOOD Mainly mice and voles,
plus some small birds and insects VOICE Shrill *kee-kee-kee*

FACT FILE

IDENTIFICATION

Most easily identified by its distinctive hovering flight, in which bird
is perfectly stationary with tail down. Male has a blue-grey head and
black-tipped tail, spotted brick-red back and black wing feathers. Female
has barred and spotted chestnut plumage with a barred, black-tipped tail
and streaked head. Juvenile resembles a heavily streaked female.
Note upright posture of perched bird, with tail noticeably longer than
closed wings.

MALE

LOCATION	DATE/TIME

STATUS AND HABITS

Commonly seen around Britain, not least because it favours roadside verges for hunting – in particular, Kestrels are seen hovering prominently above the broad, sloping motorway verges that are good habitats for their main mammal prey. In direct flight the bird has shallow and fast wingbeats, with the long tail a prominent feature. Widely distributed across Britain, including the Highlands and Islands of Scotland, although currently experiencing a population decline. Most nests are found at least semi-covered in old building recesses and cliffs. Sometimes a tree-hole nester.

KEY FACT

A hovering kestrel 20m above the ground relies on its powerful visual acuity, and can see, swoop down on and grab a mouse or vole more than 50m away.

FEMALE

PHEASANT
Phasianus colchicus

FACT FILE

SIZE Length 53–89cm **HABITAT** Farmland, woodland, large gardens **FOOD** Varied vegetable matter, including berries, tubers and grass, plus some invertebrates **VOICE** Far-carrying, crowing *korrk-korrk*

IDENTIFICATION

Male is brightly coloured with a glossy green-blue head and a long, barred tail. Scarlet face wattles, ear tufts, and cream eye-ring and bill make identification easy. Purplish and coppery plumage is heavily scalloped black, and short, round brown wings have cream feather streaks. Female is duller, with buff-brown streaked and barred plumage and a shorter tail.

> **KEY FACT** In the breeding season, the loud and repeated crowing of the male bird is accompanied by a wing-whirring jump, creating an impressive display and ensuring conspicuousness even amongst tall crops.

MALE

LOCATION	DATE/TIME

STATUS AND HABITS

Introduced to Britain from E Asia, Pheasants are now common and widespread. Absent only from the mountainous regions of Wales and N and W Scotland, they are a common sight throughout the countryside, most often encountered in open farmland and on woodland edges. Many pheasants are bred in captivity and large numbers are released for shooting. Their population is maintained at a super-abundant level by artificial feeding at grain bins, where flocks – sometimes of hundreds of birds – collect in winter.

FEMALE

RED-LEGGED PARTRIDGE
Alectoris rufa

FACT FILE

SIZE Length 32–34cm **HABITAT** Dry, open farmland and heath **FOOD** Leaves, seeds, roots, occasional insects **VOICE** Strange and remarkable harsh sounds, likened to a steam engine: *wa-shack-shack*

IDENTIFICATION

Compact and colourful gamebird. Has a large flank patch, boldly striped chestnut, black and white. Face and throat are white, with a broad black necklace extending through eye and breaking into a bib of black droplets on dove-grey breast. Bill is scarlet and eye-ring pinkish red. Belly is pinkish buff, back sandy and legs red. In flight, outer tail appears bright rufous.

LOCATION	DATE/TIME

STATUS AND HABITS

Introduced to Britain from France in the 18th century, this species has established itself as a widespread farmland bird across much of S England. It is bred for shooting, and in the dry, chalky and heathland habitats of East Anglia it can be abundant. Most often seen in pairs or loose parties of a few birds. It is a restless and nervous bird, and flies with fast, whirring wingbeats interspersed with glides just above ground level.

KEY FACT

This gamebird's preference for open, bare ground enables it to run away from danger, rather than fly, and it has a surprisingly fast sprint for such a rotund bird.

GREY PARTRIDGE
Perdix perdix

FACT FILE

SIZE Length 29–31cm **HABITAT** Lowland grassland and cultivation **FOOD** Seeds, leaves, fruits, some insects in summer **VOICE** Harsh *kirr-ic, kirr-ic*; also low, clucking notes from female

IDENTIFICATION

Small, rounded gamebird with a 'no neck' appearance and small head. Plumage is brownish grey and cryptic, finely marked with buff and dark brown above, plainer grey below. Belly has a broad, inverted, dark brown horseshoe patch on a whitish background, reduced in female. Face is brick red. Rusty outer-tail feathers are seen in flight. Juvenile is browner than adult and lacks horseshoe mark.

KEY FACT The adverse effects of intensive farming on the plant and insect food of this attractive bird has caused a steep decline in its population levels.

MALE

LOCATION	DATE/TIME

STATUS AND HABITS

Grey Partridges are still widely distributed across mainland Britain, but absent from some **N** and **W** islands. They prefer mixed farmland with plentiful nutritious foodplants and, in summer, insects for their chicks, and avoid the wettest and driest habitats. They use fieldside tracks for dust-bathing and ditches for drinking. This species is the gamebird most prized by shooting estates, where traditional coveys of 10 or more birds gather together, noticeable in the bare cultivations of autumn and winter.

FEMALE

MOORHEN
Gallinula chloropus

FACT FIL

SIZE Length 32–35cm **HABITAT** Rivers, ponds and lakes, including those in urban parks **FOOD** Seeds, grass, duckweeds and other aquatic plants, earthworms, snails, tadpoles **VOICE** Loud, harsh *krreck* and rhythmic *kipp, kipp*

IDENTIFICATION
Looks all black with a red face shield and yellow tip to red bill. Tail is constantly flicked up, revealing a black and white pattern underneath. Has a white line along flanks. In good light, back appears brownish black with slate-grey underparts. Legs and feet are green. Young birds are browner than adults, with paler flanks and chest, and white chin and throat; bill lacks bright colours.

KEY FACT
Moorhens use the water's surface for their fluttering take-off, which belies their strong flying skills. Some birds are migratory and can turn up on far-flung islands away from significant water bodies.

ADULTS FIGHTING

LOCATION	DATE/TIME

STATUS AND HABITS

Moorhens are widespread and common in Britain, occurring on many types of water body. They can often be seen in towns, strolling around mown grass near park lakes. Nests are sited in waterside vegetation, sometimes above the water level, requiring the birds to use their strong climbing skills. Territorial disputes are

settled by fights, with birds calling noisily and lashing out with their strong legs and feet as they sit back flapping on the water's surface.

LAPWING
Vanellus vanellus

SIZE Length 28–31cm **HABITAT** Wet grassland,
fields, hill pastures **FOOD** Mainly invertebrates, including worms,
beetle larvae and crane-flies **VOICE** Characteristic shrill, whistling
peeoo-wit

IDENTIFICATION

Large wader with medium-length legs. Adult has glossy green upperparts,
a broad black bib and white underparts except for a chestnut undertail,
seen when bird dips head to feed. In flight, pied underside pattern is
conspicuous, with blackish flight feathers and tail, and white body. Has
long, rounded wings, broader and longer in the male. Long head crest,
blowing in the wind, is an obvious field mark.

LOCATION	DATE/TIME

STATUS AND HABITS

Distributed across much of Britain, in both upland and lowland habitats, the Lapwing is our most commonly encountered breeding wader. In winter, it gathers around estuaries and coasts, often in large flocks with other shorebirds. The breeding display is an impressive acrobatic twisting and turning flight above its nesting fields, with birds showing off their pied wings to best effect. The species' call gives it its old English name of Peewit.

KEY FACT

Lapwings defend their young from aerial predators with a highly active mobbing flight that includes a humming, beating sound from vigorously flapping wings. They are tenacious, chasing off large intruders.

GOLDEN PLOVER
Pluvialis apricaria

SIZE Length 26–29cm **HABITAT** Upland moorland and bog in summer; lowland fields and estuaries in winter
FOOD Primarily insects, worms and mud-dwelling invertebrates
VOICE Mournful, whistling *tloo-ee*

SUMMER

IDENTIFICATION
Neat, plump wading bird with a short bill. Upperparts are spangled yellow and blackish brown. Summer male has a black face and underparts, with a broad white border extending down in front of closed wings. In flight, undersides of white wings contrast with black belly. Female has reduced black underparts and less distinct borders. Winter adult and juvenile have uniformly brown plumage.

KEY FACT The Golden Plover's display flight is one of the most evocative sounds in the uplands, with mournful, repeated, echoing whistles delivered from a circling, high, stiff-winged flight.

LOCATION	DATE/TIME

STATUS AND HABITS

A breeding bird of the British uplands, favouring open moorland with short heather and grassland habitats. Widespread in Scotland, including main offshore island groups, and has a strong population in the Pennines and a few pairs in Wales. Prefers a mosaic of wet and dry habitats to provide abundant insect larvae for its growing chicks. In winter, flocks of Golden Plovers are found across lowland Britain, particularly in cereal fields and pastures, often mixed in with Lapwings.

JUVENILE

CURLEW
Numenius arquata

SIZE **Length 50–60cm** HABITAT **Upland bog and moorland in summer; coasts and marshes in winter** FOOD **Insects, mud-dwelling invertebrates** VOICE **Mournful** *cour-lee* **and bubbling trill**

IDENTIFICATION

Large wading bird with a long, downcurved bill. When seen at a distance, plumage looks fairly uniform greyish brown; closer views reveal heavy streaks and mottling, paler underparts and a whitish eye-ring. In flight, upper wings appear darker towards tips, and underwings very pale grey and finely barred. A white 'V'-shaped wedge extends up back from barred tail.

LOCATION	DATE/TIME

KEY FACT

Our breeding Curlews migrate **S** and **W**, many to Ireland, while our winter population comprises birds that breed further **N** in Europe. The breeding population is in steep decline.

STATUS AND HABITS

A widespread bird across **Britain**, particularly in winter, when it can be seen anywhere around coasts and also in winter fallow fields. In summer, it nests mainly in uplands, although some pairs are still scattered through lowlands amongst mixed farmland and heathland. The bird's distinctive whistling call sounds like its common name and is one of the most evocative sounds of coastal marshes. Displaying above upland nest sites, Curlews rise and fall slowly on stiff, quivering wings while issuing a liquid, bubbling call.

COMMON GULL
Larus canus

SIZE Length 38–44cm HABITAT Coasts, freshwater lakes, marshes FOOD Marine invertebrates, fish, refuse, plus some earthworms and insects inland VOICE Shrill, whistling *kee-ya*

FACT FIL

IDENTIFICATION

Medium-sized gull with a darkish grey back and wings, these tipped black with white spots. Rest of adult plumage is white. Eye is dark, and bill and legs yellowish green. Has a neat-looking, rounded head and 'friendly' expression. In winter, shows a shawl of dark streaks behind head. Young birds have browner wings with a dark trailing edge and a black terminal band to tail.

WINTER

LOCATION	DATE/TIME

STATUS AND HABITS

The Common Gull breeds in small colonies in **N** Britain, often on rocky islets in freshwater lakes and in lochs in the uplands. In winter, it is common around our coasts and seas, as birds visit our islands from elsewhere in **N** Europe. It is smaller and neater looking than the very common Herring Gull, sitting more daintily on the water. With its smaller bill, it picks food carefully from the water's surface and selects only smaller items.

WINTER

KEY FACT   The Common Gull's call is plaintive and higher pitched than that of other gulls and is often heard in towns, where birds congregate on playing fields to feed on worms.

BLACK-HEADED GULL
Larus ridibundus

SIZE Length 38–44cm **HABITAT** Coasts, marshes, fields, urban parks **FOOD** Mainly marine invertebrates, earthworms and insects, plus some vegetable matter **VOICE** Various harsh, repeated notes, including a strident *kwarrr*

FACT FIL

IDENTIFICATION

Dark chocolate-brown hood of summer adult, and red bill and legs make identification straightforward. Pale gull with a dove-grey back and wings, these tipped with black. In flight, white body, tail and leading edge to wing give bird a pale appearance. Underwing has a grey-black patch behind white leading edge. Winter adult has a white head with dark smudges behind eye. Juvenile is browner grey.

KEY FACT   This is the gull most often seen following the plough in winter in lowland Britain, where the turning of the soil reveals their invertebrate prey.

SUMMER

LOCATION	DATE/TIME

STATUS AND HABITS

A very common bird across the whole of the British Isles in both summer and winter. Black-headed Gulls breed in very large, noisy colonies on coasts and in freshwater lakes and marshes. They are the most likely gull to be encountered regularly in our towns and cities, and are plentiful on lakes in urban parks. They group together with other smaller gull species, and like those have a dainty, buoyant flight and a slender bill used to pick up small food items.

WINTER

HERRING GULL
Larus argentatus

SIZE Length 55–67cm HABITAT Coasts, inland wetlands, refuse tips FOOD Marine invertebrates and fish, carrion, garbage VOICE Loud, wailing *kyow-kyow-kyow*

IDENTIFICATION

Large gull with a 'mean-looking' expression, a heavy, angled yellow bill with a red spot near tip, and a pale eye. Legs are pale pinkish. Upperparts are silver-grey and wingtips black with white spots. Adult plumage is acquired only after four years. Younger birds are mottled brown, with a dark bill and dark tail band, gradually becoming greyer and paler with age.

KEY FACT
Herring Gulls on coasts open shellfish by holding them in their beak, flying up high and then dropping them onto rocks below.

WINTER

LOCATION	DATE/TIME

STATUS AND HABITS

Widespread around our coasts in summer, where it breeds in colonies on grassy offshore islands and on ledges on sea cliffs. Increasingly nests on buildings in coastal towns, where it is considered a nuisance, its harsh, loud calls echoing around the streets. In winter, it is distributed widely throughout the countryside, and at dusk can be seen flying into mixed-gull roosts on inland reservoirs. This species is a regular feeder on rubbish tips.

SUMMER

FERAL PIGEON/ROCK DOVE
Columba livia

FACT FIL

SIZE Length 31–34cm **HABITAT** Towns, cities; truly wild Rock Doves occur only on remote oceanic coasts **FOOD** Grains, seeds, fresh young plant material **VOICE** Crooning *oor-roo-cooo*

IDENTIFICATION

Medium-sized blue-grey pigeon with two black bars on inner wing, white rump and purple-green gloss to neck feathers. Tail is grey with a black terminal band. Truly wild Rock Doves always sport this plumage. Artificial breeding and hybridisation in towns has created a wide variety of colour morphs, ranging from almost white birds, through reddish browns to almost black individuals.

LOCATION	DATE/TIME

STATUS AND HABITS

Probably the bird most frequently seen and engaged with by town- and city-dwellers, since urban areas hold large flocks of this species. Feral Pigeons are often absurdly tame, moving out of the path of pedestrians only at the last possible moment, and perching on the heads and shoulders of tourists with food at London landmarks. In contrast, the wild Rock Dove is restricted to our most remote N and W coasts and islands, and is a wary and fast-flying bird.

KEY FACT The spread of many different forms of the Feral Pigeon is diluting the wild Rock Dove stock and remains a threat to the latter's future across Britain and Europe.

WOODPIGEON
Columba palumbus

SIZE Length 40–42cm HABITAT Woodland, parks and gardens, agricultural fields FOOD Plant material, particularly cereals, vegetable crops and clover VOICE Rhythmic five-note *coo-oo-OO-oo-oo*

IDENTIFICATION

The largest British pigeon, plump and hefty. Has pale blue-grey upperparts, a warm pink breast and a black-tipped grey tail. In flight, shows white crescent markings at bend of wing. Adult has white neck marks below glossy green and purple patches. Head is grey with pale yellowish staring eyes. Legs are pink. Juvenile is duller and lacks the neck patches.

LOCATION	DATE/TIME

STATUS AND HABITS

One of our most widespread and common birds, the Woodpigeon occurs throughout Britain. It is a resident species, with birds moving into flocks in agricultural landscapes for the winter. These flocks can become very large concentrations of feeding birds where new crops are emerging, causing some conflict with farmers. Woodpigeons are also becoming a commoner sight at garden birdfeeders, where they have overcome their size and clumsiness to take advantage of high-quality seed food.

KEY FACT

A young Woodpigeon is called a squab. It has ugly bluish-pink flesh covered with hairy down and a wide bill, and is fed 'milk' regurgitated from the adult's crop.

STOCK DOVE
Columba oenas

SIZE Length 32–34cm HABITAT Mixed landscapes of farmland and woodland FOOD Grains, seeds, vegetable crops, clover VOICE Deep, gruff, cooing *ooow-oo*

FACT FIL

IDENTIFICATION
Smaller and neater than the Woodpigeon, with darker blue-grey plumage. Head and underparts are bluer, with broad, glossy green neck patches and a warm pink upper breast. In flight, shows surprisingly pointed wings with a black border, paler grey centre and two neat black marks near body. Grey tail has a black band. Juvenile is dull and browner than adult.

STATUS AND HABITS
Found across most of Britain, the Stock Dove is predominantly a bird of lowland landscapes, although it does venture into uplands, where old buildings can provide suitable nest sites. Farm woodlands with tall trees are a favoured habitat, where old growth contains holes for these cavity nesters. Quiet and unobtrusive, the species rarely forms large flocks as do some of its relatives. In flight, the birds' long wings beat deeply and are sometimes held out in a 'V'. They are fast flyers.

LOCATION	DATE/TIME

KEY FACT

The Stock Dove's display flight can include two or more birds flying around in graceful sweeps, gliding with wings held high, before weakly clapping them together and then perching for a bowing ritual.

COLLARED DOVE
Streptopelia decaocto

SIZE Length 31–33cm **HABITAT** Gardens, farms, orchards, town parks **FOOD** Cereal grains, seeds, fruits **VOICE** Penetrating, unmusical cooing

IDENTIFICATION

Has uniform, pale sandy-grey plumage, with a pinkish-buff head, neck and breast. Belly and undertail are paler cream. Uppertail is brown with whitish tips to outer feathers, and undertail has a broad white terminal band. Adult has a narrow black half-collar on neck, edged in white. Dark red eye is very narrowly ringed white, and slender bill is black. Juvenile is duller and lacks collar.

LOCATION	DATE/TIME

STATUS AND HABITS

Very common throughout Britain, and easily seen as it is associated with towns, habitation and farms. Pairs often perch together on roofs and telegraph wires, and their rather grating cooing moans are a common sound in our villages. Collared Doves regularly visit garden feeders to take advantage of high-quality seeds and grains, and they are effective scavengers of spilt grain in the farmyard. Their brief display involves a climbing flight, wing-clapping and a gliding descent.

KEY FACT

The Collared Dove is a relatively new arrival to the British avifauna, first recorded here only about 50 years ago. It has since spread very rapidly, filling what must have been a vacant niche.

TURTLE DOVE
Streptopelia turtur

SIZE Length 26–28cm **HABITAT** Warm woodlands, scrub, well-vegetated heathland **FOOD** Weed seeds and leaves, grains **VOICE** Rich, deep, purring *rroorrrr-rroorrrr*

FACT FIL

IDENTIFICATION

Small, smart dove with rich rufous-brown back and wings, streaked black. Head and neck are pale, warm pink with a bluish tinge to crown. Has a neck patch of narrow black and white stripes. In flight, shows grey inner wings and dusky flight feathers. Grey-brown rounded tail has narrow white edges. Eye is yellow with a deep red orbital ring, and legs are reddish.

KEY FACT Turtle Doves are in severe decline – three-quarters of the British population has been lost over the last 50 years. Intensification of agriculture is one cause, and studies in African winter habitats may reveal more.

LOCATION	DATE/TIME

STATUS AND HABITS

Turtle Doves spend the winter in Africa, coming to Britain in late spring to breed. They are distributed across the warmer S and E of England, with a few birds in Wales. The species is the quintessential summer bird of our countryside, its rich, purring calls emanating from thick scrub during warm evenings on the longest days of the year. The birds themselves are hard to see, although when they are flushed from roadsides their rapid flight and white-bordered dark tail are distinctive.

CUCKOO
Cuculus canorus

SIZE Length 32–34cm HABITAT Woodland, heaths, uplands FOOD Large caterpillars, particularly hairy species, plus occasional worms and other invertebrates VOICE Male utters familiar *cu-coo*; female has a liquid, bubbling song

IDENTIFICATION

In flight, the Cuckoo can be mistaken for a falcon or small hawk, with its chunky shoulders and long tail, but its fast, shallow, 'rowing' wingbeats are distinctive. Male is dark grey, with black and white barring on lower breast and underparts. Tail feathers are tipped and spotted white. Female is browner. Juvenile is brown with white barring.

KEY FACT Adult Cuckoos migrate back to Africa in Jul, before the host parent has completed raising their young. Juveniles follow in Aug and Sep, finding their own way instinctively.

LOCATION	DATE/TIME

STATUS AND HABITS

The song of this summer migrant is one of the best-known sounds in nature. Birds arrive in Britain from Africa in mid-Apr, and are then distributed widely across the region, reaching the far N. They use a diverse range of habitats, from uplands to reedbeds. Where they live depends on the availability of host species, in whose nests they lay their eggs. On moorland they parasitise Meadow Pipits, in marshes Reed Warblers, and in gardens Dunnocks.

BARN OWL
Tyto alba

FACT FIL

SIZE **Length 33–35cm** HABITAT **Fields, hedgerows, lowland and upland heaths** FOOD **Small rodents, small birds, occasional large insects** VOICE **Screeching and snoring noises in breeding season**

IDENTIFICATION

The whitish owl most likely seen on winter afternoons in our countryside. Adult has warm, vermiculated, pale golden upperparts and silver-white underparts. Golden plumage is dotted with tiny black spots and mottled with grey. White facial disc is heart-shaped, with black eyes and lines connecting eyes to bill. Legs are feathered white. In flight, rounded wings appear surprisingly long.

LOCATION	DATE/TIME

STATUS AND HABITS

The Barn Owl is present over much of S Britain but more thinly distributed in the N, where it is vulnerable during very cold winters. A hunting bird is a beautiful and memorable sight, with gentle, buoyant wingbeats, occasional hovers, and dramatic swoops to prey on the ground, landing with upstretched wings. The species can often be seen perched on roadside fenceposts. Barn Owls nest in cavities, usually in old buildings, where platforms and boxes can assist their choice of site.

KEY FACT

One of the most cosmopolitan bird species, the Barn Owl is found worldwide, with populations in the Americas, Africa, Asia and Australasia. It also has races on some far-flung oceanic islands.

TAWNY OWL
Strix aluco

FACT FIL

SIZE Length 37–39cm **HABITAT** Woods, forests, parks in towns with large trees **FOOD** Mammals, small birds, insects, amphibians **VOICE** Classic fluty, hooting *huit-hoouuu*; sharp *ke-wick* call

IDENTIFICATION

Medium-sized owl with a large, rounded head and no ear tufts. Plumage is a rich, warm brown, mottled, streaked and barred with black. Has prominent white lines down sides of back. Large facial disc is greyish, bordered blackish, with white eyebrows, lores and chin. Eyes are black. Legs and feet are feathered buff, and talons are strong and grey.

KEY FACT
Tawny Owls roost by day deep inside clumps of woodland trees, where they stay quiet and immobile. If the sleeping owl is discovered by small birds, large groups will gather to mob and scold it.

LOCATION	DATE/TIME

STATUS AND HABITS

A common bird of woodland throughout mainland Britain, the Tawny Owl is more likely to be heard than seen. Its familiar hooting is encountered in towns and villages, and in forests in open countryside. It is the most nocturnal of our owls, and its preference for large broadleaved trees means it stays well hidden. In early summer, the evening activity of feeding the fully grown, mobile young is accompanied by hoots and calls, allowing the birds to be seen more easily.

SHORT-EARED OWL
Asio flammeus

FACT FIL

SIZE Length 37–39cm; wingspan 95–110cm
HABITAT Moorland, open country, marshes, heaths and
coastal dunes **FOOD** Small mammals, birds and some insects
VOICE Low-pitched, hollow *boo-boo-boo*

IDENTIFICATION
A long-winged owl, yellowish buff at a distance, with a pale face and
staring, bright yellow eyes in dark pits. Upperparts are streaked with
black; underparts are warmer and paler, with a white underwing except
for black tips to flight feathers and black comma at bend of wing.
Upperwing flight feathers are golden, heavily barred black. Legs
and feet are feathered buff.

LOCATION	DATE/TIME

STATUS AND HABITS

This owl hunts by day as well as at night, and can be seen in summer over upland moors and on winter afternoons quartering marshes near the coast. Its long-winged, buoyant flight is attractive to watch. In summer, breeding birds are found across **N** Britain, while in winter our population moves to the warmer **S** and **W** and is augmented by European immigrants. Unlike most owls, the Short-eared adopts a horizontal posture when perching on fenceposts and rocks.

KEY FACT This species can be irruptive, whereby the population cycles of its main vole prey cause its population to fluctuate markedly. In good years, large numbers of **N** European birds add to our resident population.

LITTLE OWL
Athene noctua

FACT FIL

SIZE Length 21–23cm **HABITAT** Farmland with mature field and hedgerow trees **FOOD** Mainly beetles, moths, some small mammals and birds **VOICE** Hollow, rising, repeated whistle

IDENTIFICATION

Small, neat, dark owl with longish legs. Upperparts are dark brownish grey, liberally spotted and barred white. Brown crown is neatly speckled white. Underparts are paler grey, heavily streaked with brown, particularly on upper breast. Rectangular facial disc is pale grey with bright yellow eyes. In bounding flight, rounded, barred wings and short, barred tail are distinctive. Legs and feet are feathered whitish buff.

LOCATION	DATE/TIME

KEY FACT At least half the diet of this species comprises insects, and the pellets it ejects after feeding are clean, dry and glossy black from beetle wingcases.

STATUS AND HABITS

Now a widespread English and Welsh resident species, although initially artificially introduced from W Europe in the late 19th century. It prefers old farmland with large traditional hedges, and mature trees for nesting. It is a cavity nester, so gnarled, dead branches on old field oaks provide an ideal home. Although mostly nocturnal feeders, Little Owls can be seen perched on roadside telegraph poles in the early evening, and their fluty, whistling call can give away their presence.

SWIFT
Apus apus

SIZE Length 16–17cm; wingspan 42–48cm
HABITAT Aerial, over towns, villages, marshes and lakes
FOOD Insects, taken on the wing VOICE Harsh, screaming *swee-ree*

IDENTIFICATION

Long, stiff, swept-back wings, uniform brown plumage and fast, gliding flight action all distinguish this species from Swallow and martins. Wings look narrow and tail is noticeably forked. Has a small white throat patch. In bright sunlight, pale sheen to flight feathers and, in close views, grey forehead are sometimes visible. Juvenile is indistinguishable from adult.

KEY FACT The British Swift population has declined to around half the number of birds 50 years ago. This may be due to fewer insects, although studies in Africa may help to explain it further.

LOCATION	DATE/TIME

STATUS AND HABITS

A summer visitor to Britain, arriving from Africa in early May, and one of the first migrants to depart S again, in Aug. Birds are seen throughout Britain, apart from in the far N and W. Swifts are entirely aerial, sleeping, mating, feeding and drinking on the wing. They touch land only to breed, nesting in buildings, which brings them into close proximity with town-dwellers. Parties of screaming birds chase one another around our streets.

GREEN WOODPECKER
Picus viridis

SIZE Length 31–33cm **HABITAT** Open lowland woodland, parks, gardens, sandy heaths **FOOD** Ants, larvae of wood-boring insects **VOICE** Ringing laugh; sharp *kyack* alarm call

FACT FIL

FEMALE

IDENTIFICATION

Colourful, exotic-looking bird with bright green upperparts, a bright yellow rump and pale yellow underparts. Adult male has a red crown extending down nape, and a red moustachial stripe set in a black face patch. Female is similar but lacks red moustache. In flight, shows white-spotted dusky flight feathers, and dark tail with pointed central feathers. Juvenile is duller, spotted and barred white.

STATUS AND HABITS

Green Woodpeckers are found across Britain, absent only from the far N and W. Originally a woodland species, birds have adapted to more open habitats, and will often visit large gardens even in towns. They are the woodpecker most likely to be seen on the ground as they forage for their favourite food – ants. Sandy heathland habitats with plenty of anthills are favoured, where the birds' powerful, bounding flight is often accompanied by a raucous, 'laughing' call known as a yaffle.

LOCATION	DATE/TIME
-----	-----
-----	-----
-----	-----
-----	-----

JUVENILE

KEY FACT

The tongue of this species is very long and sticky. It is coiled up at the back of the mouth, and can be extended deep into ants' nests to capture the succulent larvae.

GREAT SPOTTED WOODPECKER
Dendrocopos major

FACT FIL

SIZE Length 22–23cm **HABITAT** Mature deciduous woods, parks, gardens, orchards **FOOD** Wood-boring insect larvae, spiders, occasional nestlings and eggs of small birds **VOICE** Sharp *tchick* and drumming

MALE

IDENTIFICATION

Medium-sized pied woodpecker with a strong bill. Upperparts are mostly black with large white shoulder patches and white-spotted barring on wings and tail. Crown, moustache and throat stripe are black, isolating white face patch from white underparts. Adult male has a crimson nape patch. Both sexes have a pinkish-red undertail and 'trousers'. Juvenile is similar, but less clean and with a dirty red crown.

KEY FACT In spring, the Great Spotted Woodpecker's loud drumming on the trunks of dead trees can be heard over large distances. This is not for hole excavation, but rather a territorial display-like song.

LOCATION	DATE/TIME

STATUS AND HABITS

Well distributed across Britain except for N Scotland. This is Britain's commonest woodpecker, most likely to be seen in gardens, where it visits feeders for peanuts in particular. Much more arboreal (tree loving) than the Green Woodpecker, this bird clearly shows adaptations for life in trees: it has two forward- and two backward-pointing toes for climbing, and a short, stiff tail for bracing against tree trunks. It is a hole nester, excavating the breeding cavity with its powerful bill.

JUVENILE

FEMALE

SKYLARK
Alauda arvensis

SIZE Length 18–19cm HABITAT Upland and lowland grasslands, cultivated fields FOOD Grains and seeds, plus insects for its young VOICE Warbling, fluty, melodious song flight; *chirropp* call

IDENTIFICATION
Small, thrush-sized bird with a stout bill and shortish tail. Upperparts are buff, streaked blackish brown. Crown is finely streaked, with a short, slightly erect crest. Has a buffish supercilium and a gorget of fine black streaks on paler breast. At rest, shows two pale wingbars and dark flight feathers. In flight, a broad white trailing edge to wings and white outer-tail feathers are revealed.

LOCATION	DATE/TIME

KEY FACT

Skylarks are ground nesters, preferring bare habitats adjacent to vegetation, and have been found to benefit from artificially created bare patches in fields of intensive crops.

STATUS AND HABITS

Widely distributed across all of Britain in both upland and lowland open habitats, the Skylark has nevertheless declined in number with the increasing intensification of agriculture. A bird of grassland and cultivation, it prefers wide, featureless landscapes, above which it can deliver its famous song flight. It rises on quivering wings, singing a rich medley of fluty whistles, often hovering high in the sky for many minutes. It is a resident species, moving S and W in colder winters.

SWALLOW
Hirundo rustica

FACT FIL

SIZE Length 17–19cm HABITAT Aerial, preferring old pastures, villages and open water FOOD Insects, taken on the wing VOICE Pleasant twittering warble with some scratchy notes; *chit* alarm

FEMALE

IDENTIFICATION
Long, forked tail, swept-back wings and small bill combine to form a classic Swallow shape. Upperparts are dark metallic blue, with red around bill and white tail spots. Blue extends across throat, separated cleanly from creamy underparts. In flight, black underwings contrast with white 'armpits', and black undertail shows a band of white spots. Outer-tail feathers extend into long streamers, longest in adult male.

STATUS AND HABITS
A summer visitor, arriving from its African wintering grounds in mid-Apr, and occurring right across the British Isles, even extending to the far N. It prefers traditional landscapes with established old grasslands and unkempt hedgerows, where it can find plenty of food. It is closely associated with human habitation, especially farmyards, where it will make its nest in an old barn, flying in through open windows and doorways. Pairs can be seen perched on roadside wires, twittering conversationally.

LOCATION	DATE/TIME

KEY FACT

Grazing marshes and pastures with cattle are important for this species, particularly where organic farming methods are used, as cowpats from cows untreated by chemicals have a higher insect diversity.

MALE

HOUSE MARTIN
Delichon urbica

SIZE Length 12.5cm **HABITAT** Aerial, above towns, villages and coastal cliffs **FOOD** Insects, taken in flight
VOICE Soft, sweet, twittering song; hard *chirrpp* call; *tseep* alarm

IDENTIFICATION

Neat, chubby, Swallow-like bird with metallic blackish-blue upperparts and clean silver-white underparts. Short, deeply cleft tail is black, isolated from black back by white undertail coverts and white rump. Head is blue-black down to a line level with bill, and lower face, chin and throat are bright silver-white. Legs are feathered white. Small bill is black.

LOCATION	DATE/TIME

STATUS AND HABITS

Its reliance on human habitation enables this species to be common across the whole of Britain, where it arrives in Apr after migrating from its African winter quarters. It prefers old towns and villages, where it sites loose nesting colonies on buildings, fixing its mud-cup nest under eaves. This is an adaptation from the species' original cliff-nesting behaviour, now restricted to remote areas. House Martins perch more freely than Swallows, and can regularly be seen around puddles on the ground collecting mud for nests.

KEY FACT

House Martins gather together in the autumn to move S to overwinter in Africa. Flocks are commonly seen sitting along roadside wires prior to departure.

TREE PIPIT
Anthus trivialis

SIZE Length 15cm HABITAT Open areas with trees, heathland, forest edges, upland oak woods FOOD Insects, spiders, occasionally seeds VOICE Descending, rattling song flight, with clear, piping whistles

IDENTIFICATION
Pipits are slightly larger and slimmer than Robins. This species is smart and clearly marked. Upperparts are buff-brown with black streaking. Has a brown eye-stripe and clear yellowish supercilium. Wing feathers are brown, edged cream. Tail is brown, edged white. Breast and flanks are yellowish with strong brown-black streaks; belly is whiter. Legs and feet are pink, and bill is dark with a pink base.

LOCATION	DATE/TIME

STATUS AND HABITS

The Tree Pipit is a summer visitor to Britain, returning from Africa in Apr. It is widespread, though thinly distributed, and prefers open habitats with trees, from where it launches its song flights. In the E, clear-fell areas of forestry on dry brecklands are favoured, whereas in the N and W it can be found in grazed upland oak and birch woods on steep valley sides. The short, repeated song flight is memorable, combining a dramatic parachuting drop with beautiful fluty whistles.

KEY FACT

We know little of this bird's movements once it leaves Britain in the autumn. A few recoveries of ringed birds are recorded from Portugal, a stop-over site on migration routes to West Africa.

MEADOW PIPIT
Anthus pratensis

SIZE Length 14.5cm HABITAT Open uplands, coastal **FACT FIL**
grazing marshes, heathland FOOD Insects, spiders, occasional
worms and seeds VOICE Flight song is an accelerating scale of
weak notes; thin *tsip* call

IDENTIFICATION

Not as clean or bright as the Tree Pipit. Has olive-brown upperparts with
blackish streaking, particularly prominent on crown and back, the latter
often with two indistinct buff braces. Face is dirty with an indistinct
buffish supercilium. Underparts are greyish white, sometimes with an
olive wash, and thinly streaked black. Bill is grey and legs pinkish buff.
Autumn juvenile is cleaner, with brighter, warmer plumage tones.

LOCATION	DATE/TIME

STATUS AND HABITS

A very common bird across most parts of Britain, particularly in uplands, where large expanses of poor habitat maintain populations of the species. In winter, it may be the only bird seen in W grassy hill land. In autumn, during migration time, flocks of Meadow Pipits may be encountered across lowland England, where they favour coastal fields and saltmarshes. It is an unobtrusive bird, noticed during its weak but persistent flight repeating its *tsip* call, and displaying white outer-tail feathers on landing.

KEY FACT

In uplands where the Meadow Pipit is the most common nesting species, it can be parasitised by the Cuckoo, and is sometimes seen feeding the monster youngster as it perches on heather near the nest.

PIED WAGTAIL
Motacilla alba yarrellii

SIZE Length 18cm **HABITAT** Gardens, parks, and open, human-modified habitats, often near water **FOOD** Insects, seeds **VOICE** Song is a hurried, twittering warble; hard, disyllabic *chissikk* call

FACT FIL

IDENTIFICATION

Smart, long-tailed black and white perching bird, usually seen striding and running on ground. Adult male has strong, even black upperparts and breast, a white face, and clean white fringes to wings and tail. Adult female is similar but with a grey back. In non-breeding adults, black breast is replaced by a narrow band. Juvenile is similar to female, but browner grey and with dirty plumage.

KEY FACT
The Pied Wagtail is the British race of the White Wagtail, which occurs in Europe and, occasionally, on spring migration in Britain; the White Wagtail is distinguished from the Pied by its pale grey upperparts.

SUMMER MALE

LOCATION	DATE/TIME

STATUS AND HABITS

Commonly encountered in towns and villages, the **Pied Wagtail** draws attention to itself with a bounding flight, loud call and habit of running across garden lawns to catch various small insects. It is found throughout Britain and prefers human habitation and water. As its name suggests, it wags its tail up and down as it walks. It commonly calls from perches on the roofs of buildings, and will build its nest in open cavities around houses and farmyards.

WINTER MALE

WAXWING
Bombycilla garrulus

FACT FIL

SIZE Length 18cm HABITAT Gardens and parks, particularly with berry-bearing shrubs in winter FOOD Berries, occasional insects VOICE Mostly silent, but call is a high, feeble trill

IDENTIFICATION

Starling-sized bird with a similar flight silhouette. When perched, however, it is paler and more colourful than the Starling. Plumage is warm pinkish buff, browner on back. Has a fluffy, backward-pointing crest, narrow black mask across face and black chin. Grey-black tail has a broad yellow tip, and undertail is chestnut. Closed wing feathers are black with white patches, yellow edging and bright waxy red appendages.

FEMALE

LOCATION	DATE/TIME

MALE

STATUS AND HABITS

This is an irruptive species that arrives in Britain in winter in varying numbers from its Scandinavian breeding grounds. It occurs initially up and down Britain's E coast, then moves inland throughout the winter, turning up almost anywhere. Small flocks of this exotic-looking bird can be a surprising addition to a suburban garden, feeding on both native and planted berry bushes. It is as likely to be seen in towns as in the countryside, and perches prominently.

KEY FACT

On their breeding grounds in Scandinavia, Waxwings favour old pine forests and circle around in the air catching insect food for their chicks.

WREN
Troglodytes troglodytes

FACT FIL

SIZE Length 9–10cm HABITAT Woodland, parks, gardens, old walls, hedgerows FOOD Spiders and insects, particularly moth caterpillars VOICE Very loud, shrill, trilling song; repeated *tic-tic* call

KEY FACT The male bird builds a series of nests, hidden in Ivy, old walls and other cavities; the female then lines her choice with feathers and lays her eggs.

IDENTIFICATION
Tiny round ball of a bird, with a long, slender, slightly downcurved bill and short, cocked tail. Has rich rufous-brown upperparts and paler buff-brown underparts, blackish barring, particularly on wings, flanks and tail, and indistinct white bars on primaries. Has a long, narrow creamy supercilium, and bright, dark eyes. Longish legs are light brown. The juvenile has even warmer rufous tones.

LOCATION	DATE/TIME

STATUS AND HABITS

The Wren's catholic taste in habitats means it is one of Britain's most widespread birds, occurring throughout the country wherever there is suitable cover provided by vegetation or rocks. Offshore islands have their own races of this species. Although its song is very loud, and the staccato ticking call is a common sound, the bird can be surprisingly difficult to see, as it keeps to dense cover. It stays low to the ground, flitting through vegetation in search of spiders and insects.

DUNNOCK
Prunella modularis

SIZE **Length 14.5cm** HABITAT **Woodland scrub, hedgerows, parks, gardens** FOOD **Seeds in winter, insects in summer** VOICE **Song is a lively but thin, short warble; piping *tseep* call**

FACT FIL

IDENTIFICATION

Slimmer than a sparrow, with a thin bill and longish tail. Predominantly dark brown with black streaking, fine on crown, coarse on back and flanks. Has a dark slate-grey supercilium, sides of face and breast. Belly is paler buff-grey. Rump is unstreaked dark brown and tail blackish brown. Eye is surprisingly red-brown. Legs are pinkish brown.

LOCATION	DATE/TIME

KEY FACT

Dunnocks have a complex breeding behaviour, whereby both sexes pair with more than one mate. Their territorial and sexual displays involve smart wing-snapping and chasing.

STATUS AND HABITS

Generally distributed across the British Isles, Dunnocks require the presence of vegetation more than the Wren, particularly scrub. They are resident, staying with us for the whole year, but can be difficult to identify because at first glance they look like a sparrow with a warbler's slender bill. Like the Wren, the Dunnock is unobtrusive; look for it on the ground in the shade of dense overhanging bushes, where it may be spotted quietly hopping along in search of insect prey. It flicks its wings in an agitated way.

ROBIN
Erithacus rubecula

SIZE Length 14cm HABITAT Woodlands, parks, gardens FOOD Mainly insects, spiders and earthworms, plus some vegetable matter VOICE Both sexes sing a mellow, whistled medley; sharp *tic* call

IDENTIFICATION

Adult has a well-known rounded silhouette with a largish head and brick-red face and breast. Upperparts and tail are olive-brown, with an indistinct collar of soft blue-grey separating brown from red. Flanks are buff, belly and undertail white. Eye is bright black, bill dark brown and legs brown. Juvenile plumage is warm brown and buff, heavily spotted paler and lacking red breast.

STATUS AND HABITS

Widespread across Britain, preferring wooded habitats and, unlike in Europe, found in close association with humans. One of our most familiar garden birds. Robins spend most of their time in quiet, shady places where the ground is moist and they can find plentiful invertebrate food. They nest in open cavities and are renowned for choosing interesting nest sites in old containers and corners of outbuildings. They will nest in open-fronted nestboxes. In winter, our resident population is swelled by immigrants from N Europe.

LOCATION	DATE/TIME

KEY FACT

In winter, both sexes hold territories and therefore sing to advertise the fact. When the leaves are falling and the temperature drops, the Robin's winter song sounds mournful.

NIGHTINGALE
Luscinia megarhynchos

SIZE Length 16.5cm **HABITAT** Scrub and woodland with a dense coppice understorey **FOOD** Worms, insects, fruit, berries **VOICE** Wonderful rich, varied and prolonged song with pure whistles and rattles

FACT FIL

IDENTIFICATION

Rather uniform brown chat with a rounded body shape and longish tail, sometimes cocked. Upperparts are rich brown with a warm rufous tone to rump and bright, dark-centred chestnut tail. Face is paler brown with beady black eye and narrow, pale buff eye-ring. Underparts are dirty cream-buff, with a brighter undertail. Bill is dark grey-brown with a pale yellowish base, and legs are pale.

MALE

LOCATION	DATE/TIME

KEY FACT The Nightingale's song – one of the most beautiful sounds of the countryside – is a complex set of over a hundred repeated phrases. The bird sings during the day as well as at night.

STATUS AND HABITS
Restricted to SE England, where the population is declining. A bird of dense cover, the Nightingale is difficult to see, and is renowned not for its plumage but for its song. Damp, shady woodlands are preferred, with plenty of dense understorey, such as the coppiced Hazel woods in East Anglia and Kent. The species also occurs in scrub habitats on the slopes of chalk grassland valleys, and on heathland. Very rarely seen in the open, preferring the shade under bushes to feed.

MALE

STONECHAT
Saxicola torquata

SIZE Length 12.5cm **HABITAT** Heaths, young forestry plantations, coastal dunes **FOOD** Insects, with some spiders, worms and seeds **VOICE** Song is a quiet series of scratchy whistles; hard *tsak* call

IDENTIFICATION

Smaller than a Robin. Adult male is very smart with a clean, dark brown, almost black, head and large white neck patches. Back is dark brown with a white panel on closed wing, and a streaky dark and white rump. Breast and flanks are rich, warm orange and belly is grey. Bill and legs are black. Adult female is browner, and white is replaced by buff. Juvenile is spotted.

MALE

FEMALE

LOCATION	DATE/TIME

STATUS AND HABITS

A locally common species, occurring mainly right around the coasts of Britain. The Stonechat is resident, although the population fluctuates from summer to winter. Breeding birds become less coastal in winter, moving S and inland, and immigrants from elsewhere in Europe visit our coasts. In the breeding season, when perching prominently on yellow gorse flowers, this species provides a striking and attractive spectacle. It draws attention to itself with its bouncy flight, flitting tail and flicking wings on perching.

KEY FACT

The Stonechat's common name comes from its often repeated call, like the sound of two pebbles being struck together. It is usually the first key to the bird's presence.

WHINCHAT
Saxicola rubetra

FACT FIL

SIZE Length 12.5cm HABITAT Open heathlands and meadows with scrub, Bracken in uplands FOOD Invertebrates, including occasional small snails VOICE Short, warbling song with some mimicry; *tic-tic* call

IDENTIFICATION

Same size as a Stonechat, from which it is tricky to separate in juvenile plumage. Adult male has a dark brown head, white supercilium and white border to cheek, meeting on nape. Back is dark brown, streaked blackish. Wings are dark with white bases to flight feathers. Dark tail has white sides at base. Legs and bill are black. Female and juvenile are duller buff and less distinctly marked.

MALE

LOCATION	DATE/TIME

STATUS AND HABITS

A long-distance migrant, the Whinchat is in Britain only between Apr and Sep. Although distributed quite widely across Britain, it is now found most commonly in upland areas of the N and W, and is seen around the coasts on passage in spring and autumn. It prefers dry grasslands and heathy vegetation with plenty of tall plants for perching, and is increasingly favouring Bracken-covered hillsides, which are spreading in upland valleys. It perches prominently, including on fences and telegraph wires.

FEMALE

KEY FACT

Whinchats are visual feeders, using a prominent perch from which to drop down onto their insect prey. They are active well into the evening, and so are described as crepuscular.

REDSTART
Phoenicurus phoenicurus

FACT FIL

SIZE Length 14cm **HABITAT** Open deciduous woods, including upland oak woods **FOOD** Insects, particularly caterpillars **VOICE** Song is a short, melancholy warble, rich-toned and rattling; soft *hweet* or liquid *twickk* call

IDENTIFICATION

One of our smartest woodland birds. Its size and shape recall a Robin, but with a longer, shivered orange-red tail. Adult male is blue-grey above with dusky wings, orange below. Has a white forehead and black face and throat. Bill and legs black. Female is browner and lacks face markings, but retains orange-buff underparts and striking orange tail. Juvenile has an adult-like tail but is otherwise speckled buff-brown.

MALE

LOCATION	DATE/TIME

KEY FACT Like many of our long-distance migrants, the Redstart is declining steeply in number. Work is underway to understand whether climate change is affecting these birds in winter and on migration.

FEMALE

STATUS AND HABITS

Redstarts migrate to Britain from Africa, arriving in Apr and departing again by the end of Sep. They are mostly absent from lowland E England, preferring N and W woods, including sparse oak and birch in the uplands. There is, however, a strong population in the New Forest. Although colourful, they can be hard to spot amongst dense green foliage, and their song is short and quite weak. The bird's shivering red tail, seen when it perches on low branches in the shade, is often the best clue to its presence.

BLACK REDSTART
Phoenicurus ochruros

SIZE Length 14.5cm HABITAT Brownfield sites in cities, buildings, rocky coasts on migration FOOD Insects, with some berries in autumn VOICE Song is a short, weak, scratchy warble; short *tsip* call

IDENTIFICATION

Adult male is predominantly dusky slate grey with a black face and breast. Has dusky brown wings with a prominent whitish panel. Vent and undertail are orange. Rump and tail are rich chestnut-orange, centre and tips dark brown. Bill and legs are black. Female is dull grey-brown, retaining red tail but lacking wing panel. Autumn male resembles female. Juvenile is like female, and speckled.

MALE

LOCATION	DATE/TIME

JUVENILE

KEY FACT

Black Redstart numbers have increased in England since the birds first bred here at the beginning of the 20th century. Our warming climate may provide suitable conditions for their continuing spread.

STATUS AND HABITS

Small numbers of this migrant species breed in and around selected towns in **SE** England. In London, Black Redstarts prefer brownfield sites with plenty of waste ground and weedy vegetation. The males defend territories by singing from the roofs of tall buildings. Britain is at the **N** edge of the species' range; elsewhere in Europe it is commonly found in villages, particularly in mountainous areas, where it also favours rocky slopes. In Oct, migrating individuals arrive around our coasts.

BLACKBIRD
Turdus merula

SIZE Length 24–25cm **HABITAT** Woodland, parks and   **FACT FIL**
gardens, towns, moorland **FOOD** Fruit, berries, seeds, earthworms,
slugs, insects **VOICE** Rich, fluty song, ending conversationally; call is a
shrill chatter; thin *seee* alarm

IDENTIFICATION

One of our most familiar birds. Adult male is completely glossy black with
a bright golden-yellow bill and narrow yellow eye-ring. Has a long, broad
tail and strong, dark brown legs. Female is dark brown, with paler, warmer
tones on underparts, dark blackish mottling on breast and a dark bill.
Juvenile resembles rufous female, spotted and speckled with orangey buff.

MALE

LOCATION	DATE/TIME

STATUS AND HABITS

Distributed across the British Isles, and one of our commonest and most frequently seen species. Blackbirds frequent a wide variety of habitats, including sites in towns and cities, where they are a popular and ever-present garden visitor. In N and W uplands and islands, they also occur in open habitats with a few trees. The scolding, chattering call is commonly heard as birds are disturbed during woodland walks, and their habit of hopping around garden lawns searching for earthworms makes them readily visible.

FEMALE

KEY FACT

In autumn and winter, the British population of Blackbirds is swelled by an influx of migrant individuals from Scandinavia, which feed in flocks on bushes with abundant berries. Both sexes of these birds have a black bill.

REDWING
Turdus iliacus

SIZE Length 21cm HABITAT Woodland, scrub, hedgerows, gardens, also on stubble in winter FOOD Berries, fruit, insects, worms VOICE High-pitched, far-carrying, thin *seee-ip* call

FACT FIL

IDENTIFICATION

Neat, smallish thrush, with plumage similar to a Song Thrush. Differs from that species in having a long cream supercilium, and bright red flanks and underwing coverts. Upperparts are dark brown. Breast is warm buff with thick blackish streaking, and rest of underparts are white, neatly streaked brown. Bill is dark with yellowish base and legs are flesh-brown. Juvenile is buff around face and has darker streaking on underparts.

LOCATION	DATE/TIME

STATUS AND HABITS

A widespread winter visitor to Britain, arriving in flocks from Scandinavia in autumn. A very few pairs breed here annually, mainly in N Scotland. During the autumn and winter, large flocks of mixed species of 'winter thrushes', including Redwings, are encountered throughout the countryside. Their feeding activity varies between ground-based searching of grassland and stubble for worms and insects, and raiding berry bushes in hedgerows. During cold spells Redwings visit gardens and orchards for fallen fruit.

KEY FACT

Redwings are night migrants. On clear, cold evenings in Oct, it is possible to detect migrating flocks in our skies, as groups continuously make their thin, whistling calls while flying over.

FIELDFARE
Turdus pilaris

SIZE **Length 25.5cm** HABITAT **Woodland, parks, gardens, orchards, also winter stubble** FOOD **Worms, insects, berries, fruit, grain** VOICE **Strong, rattling** *tchak tchak*

FACT FIL

IDENTIFICATION

Large, bulky, long-tailed thrush. Adult has a slate-grey head, neck and rump, contrasting with chestnut back and black tail. Chin is white, and throat and breast warm yellow-brown, streaked black. Belly and undertail are greyish white, marked with heavy blackish chevrons. In flight, shows a bright white underwing. Bill is yellow with a black tip and legs are dark. Juvenile is paler and speckled.

LOCATION	DATE/TIME

KEY FACT

Large flocks of Fieldfares seek out orchards with plenty of fallen fruit on which to feed. These noisy, wheeling flocks give away their presence and distinguish them from other thrushes, which are often quiet, unobtrusive birds.

STATUS AND HABITS

Along with the Redwing, this species is a common and widespread winter visitor to Britain, arriving in flocks from N Europe in autumn. One or two pairs occasionally stay to breed, mainly in N England. Fieldfares have a strong, bounding flight with flaps and glides, and call as they fly, their hard, repeated *tchak*-ing note one of the

characteristic late-autumn sounds of our farmed landscape. They mix with other thrushes in flocks that strip winter berries from hedgerows.

SONG THRUSH
Turdus philomelos

SIZE Length 23cm HABITAT Woodland, parks, gardens, commonly in towns FOOD Earthworms, snails, insects, fallen fruit, berries VOICE Song comprises clear, fluty phrases, repeated two or three times; quiet *sipp* call

IDENTIFICATION

Familiar thrush with neat proportions, warm brown upperparts, buff underparts that are heavily spotted black, and a rich yellow-brown wash across breast. Black spotting is arranged in lines. Rump is olive-brown, and crown and tail are slightly rufous. Face has a cream moustache, black stripe next to white throat and pale eye-ring. Underwings are orange-buff. Juvenile is similar, with pale buff streaks on back.

STATUS AND HABITS

Distributed throughout the British Isles, although the population is declining; now as likely to be encountered in gardens and town parks as in the countryside. On some island groups, birds can be very confiding. On the ground, its posture is upright and its movement is either a short run followed by a pause, or a series of hops. Birds listen for worms, motionless and with their head held to one side. In suburbs with trees, the Song Thrush's repetitive, strong song is a loud reminder of nature.

LOCATION	DATE/TIME

KEY FACT

Well known for its habit of cracking open snails, one of its preferred foods. It beats the snail shells against a chosen rock, called an anvil, and then extracts the juicy prize.

MISTLE THRUSH
Turdus viscivorus

SIZE **Length 27cm** HABITAT **Woodland with tall, mature trees, parks, gardens** FOOD **Fruit, berries, insects, worms** VOICE **Song comprises short, clipped, rich, fluty phrases; call is a harsh rattle**

FACT FIL

IDENTIFICATION

Large, bulky, long-tailed greyish thrush. Upperparts are cold grey-brown, underparts are whitish and covered in randomly arranged, large black spots. Flanks and breast sport a warm yellowish wash. Note distinctive white tips to outer-tail feathers and pale bar on closed wing. Bright white underwing is visible in flight. Juvenile is much more spotted, and is speckled above.

LOCATION	DATE/TIME

STATUS AND HABITS

Found across Britain in most habitats with trees, preferring stands of tall, mature broadleaved species in which to site its nest high up in a branch fork. More thinly distributed in the **N** and **W** of Scotland. Mistle Thrushes do visit gardens, but are less urbanised than the Song Thrush. In winter, they join other thrushes to forage in stubble fields and to raid hedgerow berry bushes. The species' loud, rattling call and bounding flight are good identification features.

KEY FACT The Mistle Thrush delivers its clipped but rich and powerful song from high in the boughs of a tree during windy and wet spring weather. This behaviour has earned it the alternative common name of Storm-cock.

GARDEN WARBLER
Sylvia borin

SIZE Length 14cm **HABITAT** Dense, thick undergrowth in broadleaved woodland **FOOD** Insects, berries **VOICE** Song is a rich, even, long, flowing warble; hard *tacc* and grating *churr* calls

IDENTIFICATION
Compact, plump warbler, plain buff-brown with few distinguishing plumage features. Has brown upperparts, darker on wings and tail, with pale buff underparts, whiter on belly and undertail. Head is rounded, with a plain face, narrow, pale eye-ring and stubby black bill. Legs and feet are dark grey-brown. Juvenile has warmer tones to plumage.

LOCATION	DATE/TIME

STATUS AND HABITS

A fairly late-arriving migrant from Africa, seen and heard in Britain from late Apr. Generally distributed across S Britain, thinning out in S Scotland and absent as a breeding species from the far N. Skulking and secretive, with often the only clue to its presence being the pleasant, sustained, liquid, warbling song delivered from deep inside scrubby bushes. When first seen, the bird's rather featureless appearance can leave the observer wondering how to identify it correctly.

KEY FACT

In the absence of any really striking plumage features, the Garden Warbler has become a favourite for its persistent, rich, even song, which some say rivals that of the Nightingale.

LESSER WHITETHROAT
Sylvia curruca

SIZE Length 12.5–13.5cm HABITAT Hedgerows, dense scrub FOOD Insect larvae, spiders, berries in autumn VOICE Song is a loud, rattling repetition on one note, ending suddenly; hard *tacc tacc* call

FACT FIL

IDENTIFICATION

Smart and neat, though fairly monochrome, warbler. Upperparts are dull grey-brown and underparts dirty buff, with a very pale pinkish wash in some adult males. Head and face are dark slate grey, smartly demarcated from clean white throat. Has black between eye and bill, and dark tail with white outer feathers. Bill is blackish, eye is pale brown and legs are dark grey.

LOCATION	DATE/TIME

STATUS AND HABITS

A summer migrant, arriving in late Apr and May, the Lesser Whitethroat is more or less confined to England and Wales as a breeding bird, and is seen elsewhere only on passage. It frequents dense thickets of vegetation, its distinctive rattling song usually emanating from deep within impenetrable bushes. Despite its rather monochrome plumage, it is a smart bird with a welcoming and pleasant voice. Later in the season, when adults have young, their hard, scolding calls can be persistent.

KEY FACT

This species is unusual amongst our long-distance migrants in that it heads off in a SE direction in autumn to overwinter in East Africa. Most other migrants travel through the Iberian Peninsula to West Africa.

WHITETHROAT
Sylvia communis

FACT FIL

SIZE Length 14cm **HABITAT** Open habitats with scrub, heathlands, sand-dunes, hedgerows **FOOD** Insects and their larvae, berries **VOICE** Song is a short, rapid, scratchy warble; scolding *charr* call

IDENTIFICATION
More colourful than the Lesser Whitethroat, with greys enlivened by a rufous wing panel and pinkish-buff underparts. Adult male has a grey head with a white eye-ring and brown eye, and bright white chin and throat. Back is brownish grey and longish tail dark, edged with white. Bill is brown, tipped dark. Legs and feet are pale flesh-brown. Female and juvenile are duller with a dirty white throat.

LOCATION	DATE/TIME

STATUS AND HABITS

A summer visitor, arriving in Britain from early Apr. It is a common warbler, encountered throughout the countryside where there are suitable hedgerows and other scrubby, open habitats. It is commonest in England and Wales, also breeding in S and central Scotland but generally absent from the far N. The Whitethroat draws attention to itself by its perky song, often delivered from a short, haphazard song flight above a roadside hedge. When nesting, it will scold intruders from a prominent perch.

KEY FACT

The Whitethroat population has recovered from a crash some decades ago. This was caused by a persistent drought in its Sahelian wintering grounds in West Africa, which made it difficult for birds to fatten for their arduous migration.

JUVENILE

BLACKCAP
Sylvia atricapilla

FACT FIL

SIZE **Length 13cm** HABITAT **Coppiced woodland, scrub, parks, bushy gardens** FOOD **Insects, fruit, berries** VOICE **Song is a bright, bouncy, rich warble; harsh *tacc* call**

IDENTIFICATION

Adult male is a grey-brown warbler with a neat black cap extending down to eye. Upperparts are ashy brown, darker on wings and tail. Underparts are silvery grey, whiter on belly and undertail. Bill is dark and legs slate grey. Female is warmer brown with a bright red-brown cap. Juvenile is similar to female but with a duller brown cap.

MALE

LOCATION	DATE/TIME

STATUS AND HABITS

One of our earliest summer migrants, arriving from the S at the end of Mar. Found commonly throughout most of the British Isles, though more thinly distributed and local in N Scotland. A common passage migrant around coasts. Spring woodlands are enlivened by the Blackcap's song, which is a loud, fluty warble, uneven in delivery and rising in pitch. The male sings from thick undergrowth, although the species is less skulking than its relatives. A familiar bird, also seen in town parks.

FEMALE

KEY FACT

The British breeding population migrates to S Europe and North Africa; the increasing trend of individuals wintering in Britain is explained by other birds coming here from colder areas of N Europe.

WILLOW WARBLER
Phylloscopus trochilus

FACT FIL

SIZE **Length 10.5–11.5cm** HABITAT **Forests, woods (including young conifer plantations), shelter belts** FOOD **Insect larvae, spiders, berries in autumn** VOICE **Song is a cascade of sweet, warbling notes; *hoo-eet* call**

IDENTIFICATION

Small and slim, olive-green above and yellowish white below. Has a pale yellow supercilium, brown bill and orange-brown legs. Adult plumage becomes browner with wear. Juvenile is brighter green and yellow. The song – a sweet, descending scale of notes – conclusively separates this species from the almost identical-looking Chiffchaff.

KEY FACT In Britain, the Willow Warbler's range is changing: populations are shrinking in S England and growing in Scotland. Upland conifer plantations are newly favoured, and climate change may be driving the move N.

LOCATION	DATE/TIME

STATUS AND HABITS

Like most warblers in Britain, this species is a summer migrant that arrives in Apr. It is widespread and common, occupying a diverse range of habitats where there are trees. As Willow Warblers set up territory in spring, favoured habitats seem full of the sound of their song. Warblers of the genus *Phylloscopus* are insect-eaters, mainly feeding on small caterpillars gleaned from the leaves of tall trees. They are continuously active, flicking their wings while moving through the foliage.

CHIFFCHAFF
Phylloscopus collybita

SIZE Length 10–11cm HABITAT Broadleaved
woodland, copses, hedgerows FOOD Insects and their larvae,
spiders VOICE Diagnostic song, comprising two repeated notes, *chiff-chaff*; *hweet* call

FACT FIL

IDENTIFICATION

Very similar to the Willow Warbler, though generally duller. Brownish olive
above, and dirty, pale yellow-buff below, shading to greyish white on belly
and undertail. Dirty greenish-yellow wash on sides of breast below
shoulders and thin, pale yellow supercilium are the only noticeable
plumage features. Legs are
dark. Juveniles are brighter,
with warmer brown upperparts
and yellowish underparts.

STATUS AND HABITS

The first migrant warbler to
arrive in Britain, in mid-Mar.
Common and widespread
throughout S England and
Wales, thinning out further N
and absent as a breeding bird
in N Scotland. Birds spend the
winter in S Europe and North
Africa, with a few individuals
nowadays choosing to stay in
Britain. Like the Willow
Warbler, this bird's song is
key to its identification. The
thin, repeated, two-note
whistles of its name echo
around the sparsely leafed
trees of early spring.

LOCATION	DATE/TIME

KEY FACT

Other forms of Chiffchaff also occur occasionally in Britain. In late autumn greyer visitors from Siberia stop by on passage, and in spring the Iberian Chiffchaff is now increasingly heard.

GOLDCREST
Regulus regulus

FACT FIL

SIZE Length 9cm **HABITAT** Coniferous woods, gardens, plus scrub in autumn and winter **FOOD** Spiders, insects **VOICE** Song is a thin, repeated, rising, accelerating trill; call is very high-pitched *tsee-tsee-tsee*

IDENTIFICATION
Tiny – the smallest British bird. Dull olive-green, paler on underparts. Green wing coverts give way to a pale wingbar and whitish wing panel on short, pointed wings. Has a plain face with a short black moustache and beady black eye, and black lateral crown stripes either side of orange-yellow centre crown stripe. In female, centre crown stripe is paler yellow. Juvenile lacks crown markings.

MALE

LOCATION	DATE/TIME

KEY FACT In winter, Goldcrests commonly join mixed flocks of tits and Treecreepers, moving through the canopy in search of food. They can be detected by their very thin, high-pitched, repeated calls.

FEMALE

STATUS AND HABITS

A common resident throughout Britain except the far NW. In addition, migrant birds from N Europe move down our coasts in autumn. Goldcrests nest in conifer woods and have benefited from young conifer plantations across the N uplands. Further S, they are found in villages and churchyards, where old Common Yew trees are their preferred habitat. Although Goldcrests are tiny and unobtrusive, they can be easy to see, unconcerned by human presence as they feed, hovering prominently around the tips of low-level branches.

FIRECREST
Regulus ignicapillus

SIZE **Length 9cm** HABITAT **Broadleaved and conifer** FACT FILE
woodlands, parks FOOD **Small insects, spiders, plus their larvae
and eggs** VOICE **Song is a rapid series of evenly pitched and timed
notes;** *zit* **call**

IDENTIFICATION

Same size as the Goldcrest, with similar plumage but more brightly
coloured. Has a boldly striped head with a black-bordered golden-orange
crown stripe, and a broad white supercilium and dark eye-stripe. Its face
pattern gives the bird a very different look from the Goldcrest. Upperparts
are bright olive-green, underparts silvery grey. Shoulders have rich bronzy
patches. Female is duller. Juvenile lacks orange in crown.

MALE

LOCATION	DATE/TIME

STATUS AND HABITS

Increasingly colonising parts of S England as a breeding bird, at the N edge of its European range. Semi-colonial, with concentrations of breeding pairs occurring in the New Forest and East Anglia. Firecrests are migratory, moving S and W in winter, when our population is swelled by visitors from Continental Europe. Less tied to conifers than the Goldcrest – can be found in mature Beech woods in summer and favours urban churchyards in coastal towns in autumn.

KEY FACT

Firecrests are found in mixed flocks with Goldcrests, tits and Treecreepers in late autumn. Persistent searching by the keen observer can often result in spectacular close-up views of this tiny gem.

MALE

PIED FLYCATCHER
Ficedula hypoleuca

SIZE **Length 13cm** HABITAT **Open deciduous and
mixed woodlands, including upland oak woods** FOOD **Insects,
especially their larvae** VOICE **Repetitive, short song ending in a trill;
sharp *pwheet* call** FACT FIL

IDENTIFICATION

Breeding male is essentially black above and clean white below. White
forehead and broad white wing patch relieve the black above, and has
white outer-tail feathers. After breeding, moult replaces black with dull
brown, though darker rump and tail remain, so that male resembles
female. Juvenile is speckled above. Bill and legs are black in all plumages.
Sits quietly, flicking its wings and tail.

MALE

LOCATION	DATE/TIME

STATUS AND HABITS

A summer migrant, arriving
from Africa at the end of Apr.
Distributed across W and N Britain
only, and absent as a breeding
species from the S and E. Males
arrive first, select the nest site and
sing until they have attracted a
female. They choose prominent
perches, either at the top of a
woodland tree, or on a branch near
the nest-hole. During autumn
migration, when all plumages are
grey-brown and white, Pied
Flycatchers occur on the coast.

FEMALE

KEY FACT

The Pied Flycatcher is a long-distance migrant that is
showing a marked population decline. Fortunately, these hole-nesters
have readily accepted nestboxes, and organised nestbox schemes have
increased breeding numbers locally.

SPOTTED FLYCATCHER
Muscicapa striata

SIZE Length 14.5cm HABITAT Woodland edges, parks, gardens FOOD Insects, taken mainly on the wing VOICE Song comprises a few quiet, squeaky notes; sharp *tzee-tzucc* call

IDENTIFICATION

Long-tailed grey flycatcher whose large eyes give it a 'friendly' appearance. Upperparts are uniform grey-brown, and underparts are whitish, streaked brown and with a buff-brown wash on flanks. Crown is neatly and finely streaked black, and has a very narrow, pale eye-ring. Largish bill is black, legs are dark brown. Juvenile is buffer with pale flecking.

LOCATION	DATE/TIME

STATUS AND HABITS

A long-distance migrant, arriving in Britain from Africa late in spring (from mid-May). The Spotted Flycatcher is widely but thinly distributed throughout Britain. It often associates with humans, preferring large, mature gardens and farmsteads with plenty of tall trees and insects. It catches its prey by repeated sallies from a prominent perch on telephone wires, fenceposts or exposed tree branches. Ivy-covered walls are favoured nest sites, as this species prefers crevices with some protective cover.

KEY FACT

The European population of this species is in rapid decline. Work is underway to study its ecological requirements on migration and in its wintering grounds in West Africa.

CRESTED TIT
Lophophanes cristatus

SIZE Length 11.5cm **HABITAT** Native pine forest

FOOD Insects and their larvae, pinecone seeds, berries

VOICE Call is a low-pitched, purring trill, repeated in song

IDENTIFICATION

Small tit with a striking backward-pointed black and white crest. Adult has a white face with a black line curving from eye around cheek. Another black line curves down from rear of crest around sides of neck to join neat black bib. Upperparts are grey-brown and underparts orange-buff. Bill is black and legs grey. Juvenile has a shorter crest.

LOCATION	DATE/TIME

STATUS AND HABITS

The Crested Tit is a sedentary resident with a highly restricted range in Britain. It is a Scottish speciality, confined to native Scots Pine forest in the Spey Valley and reaching coastal woodlands E of Inverness. Like most tits, it is a confiding bird, though its unobtrusive habits and small population make it quite difficult to see. It will visit feeders in gardens close to native pine trees, and also forages for insects and spiders, Treecreeper-like, up and down the trunks of old trees.

KEY FACT

The Crested Tit is our most sedentary bird, very rarely recorded away from its restricted breeding range. It needs rotten wood in which to excavate a nest-hole.

COAL TIT
Periparus ater

SIZE Length 11.5cm **HABITAT** Coniferous forest and woodland, parks and gardens with conifers **FOOD** Insects, spiders, seeds **VOICE** Loud, repeated *teechu-teechu* song; sharp *tseee* call **FACT FIL**

IDENTIFICATION

Small, short-tailed tit. Adult has a black head, white cheeks and a diagnostic white nape patch. A black bib extends from chin to upper breast. Upperparts are dark olive-grey, with two short white wingbars and a pale wing panel. Underparts are warm orange-buff, richest on flanks and sides of breast. Has a fine black bill and slate-grey legs. Juvenile is similar but less distinctively marked.

KEY FACT
In winter, this species joins with other tits, crests and Treecreepers in mixed foraging flocks, when it can sometimes be seen running along the high branches of pine trees.

LOCATION	DATE/TIME

STATUS AND HABITS

A widespread and common resident, found throughout Britain. Prefers conifer woodlands, but not exclusively, and is regularly found in large gardens, cemeteries and parks with firs and Common Yew. It is an acrobatic tit, perching or hanging on the ends of branches to glean insects and spiders, or extracting seeds from pinecones. The white nape patch can be difficult to see, but the white wingbars are conspicuous lines of white spots. A hole-nester, the Coal Tit readily occupies nestboxes.

LONG-TAILED TIT
Aegithalos caudatus

SIZE Length 14cm **HABITAT** Deciduous woodland, parks, gardens, hedgerows **FOOD** Insects, spiders, plus some seeds and buds **VOICE** Rippling, trilling *tsirrupp* call, repeated as a limited song

FACT FIL

IDENTIFICATION
Unmistakable tit with a tiny, round, fluffy body and very long tail. Impression is of a pale bird, with a dirty whitish head and underparts washed with pink on nape, belly and flanks. Has a dark smudge above eye from bill to neck, blackish upperparts with pink shoulders, and a white panel in wing. Tail is black with prominent white edges. Eye-ring is reddish and tiny bill black.

STATUS AND HABITS
A common and widespread resident found throughout Britain except in the very far **NW** of Scotland. Prefers areas with plenty of trees and scrub, requiring dense undergrowth to conceal its nest. Out of the breeding season, this species is gregarious and social, flocks moving together and calling to one another conversationally. Birds are surprisingly acrobatic, and flocks regularly attend garden feeding stations in the winter, taking seeds and nuts. It is a weak flyer, with whirring wings. Roosts communally at night, huddled in dense vegetation.

LOCATION	DATE/TIME

KEY FACT

The Long-tailed Tit's nest is an amazing hollow, oval structure of woven mosses and cobwebs, lined on the outside with lichens. An entrance hole is concealed near the top.

GREAT TIT
Parus major

SIZE Length 14cm **HABITAT** Deciduous woodland, parks, gardens, towns, cities **FOOD** Insects (particularly caterpillars), seeds, nuts, buds **VOICE** Song is a loud, repeated *tee-cher, tee-cher*; variety of metallic ringing calls

IDENTIFICATION

Large, bulky, strikingly coloured tit. Adult has a glossy black head and bib, framing white cheeks. Upperparts are bright yellow-green, and wings blackish with a strong white wingbar and pale wing panel. Longish tail is black with white outer feathers. Underparts are bright lemon yellow with a broad black stripe down centre, extending further between legs in male. Has a strong black bill and slaty legs. Juvenile is browner with paler yellow.

LOCATION	DATE/TIME

STATUS AND HABITS

A very common and widely distributed bird, found as a resident throughout Britain except for local absences in parts of N Scotland. Originally a bird of broadleaved woodland, the Great Tit is now a ubiquitous inhabitant of town and city parks and gardens. In the breeding season, it is highly vocal, singing its repetitive two-note song from a prominent perch high in the trees. The species is a constant visitor to garden feeding stations year-round.

KEY FACT Great Tits are hole-nesters, though much more catholic than most of their relatives in choice of nest site. Nests have been found in a wide variety of discarded man-made receptacles.

BLUE TIT
Cyanistes caeruleus

FACT FIL

SIZE **Length 11.5cm** HABITAT **Woodland, city parks, gardens, orchards** FOOD **Insects and their larvae, fruit, buds, seeds** VOICE **Song is a quick** *tsee-tsee-tsee-tsuhuhu* **crescendo;** *chirr-r-r* **alarm**

IDENTIFICATION

Our only familiar blue-coloured garden bird. Adult has a bright blue crown and a white face with a neat black stripe through eye, connected around cheek with blackish chin-strap. Back is yellowish green, and wings and tail blue. Underparts are bright yellow with a small, isolated, central black stripe. Short bill is silver grey and legs slate blue. Juvenile is washed yellow and has less blue.

LOCATION	DATE/TIME

STATUS AND HABITS

Abundant and widespread resident species throughout Britain wherever there are trees. It prefers broadleaved trees, where it commonly forages high up in the canopy during the breeding season, gleaning small caterpillars from leaves to feed to its large broods of chicks. This hole-nester is the most regular user of artificial nestboxes in gardens. Blue Tits are common garden birds and are regularly seen at feeding stations, where they take seeds, nuts and fat. They are highly acrobatic, often seen feeding at the tips of small branches.

KEY FACT
The presence of Blue Tits in your garden can be ascertained by observing a bird table. Ringing studies have shown that even a small urban garden may attract more than 50 birds if food is put out regularly.

MARSH TIT
Poecile palustris

SIZE Length 11.5cm **HABITAT** Woodland, including gardens with trees **FOOD** Insects, seeds, berries
VOICE Repetitive, single-note song; distinctive *pitch-uu* call

IDENTIFICATION
Difficult to separate visually from the Willow Tit. Adult is buff-brown with a glossy black cap from bill to nape, white cheeks and a small black bib. Upperparts are grey-brown, and underparts dirty white with a dull buff wash to flanks and undertail. Bill is short and black, legs are dull slate. Juvenile is similar but has a dull cap.

LOCATION	DATE/TIME

STATUS AND HABITS

A S resident in Britain, common and widespread in England and Wales, though its distribution thins out in the W. Absent from Scotland, where it is replaced by the Willow Tit. Despite its name, it is not a bird of marshes, preferring deciduous woods, including dry oak and Beech as well as riverine stands of Common Alders. Spends less time in the canopy than other tits and more time in low, dense vegetation. In some areas it regularly visits garden feeders for seeds and nuts.

KEY FACT

The glossy black cap, small bib and lack of a pale wing panel help to distinguish this species from the Willow Tit. Its distinctive, explosive call is diagnostic.

WILLOW TIT
Poecile montanus

FACT FIL

SIZE Length 11.5cm HABITAT Damp woodland, including birch and conifers FOOD Insects, spiders, berries VOICE Song is a repeated single note; thin eez-eez and nasal *tchay* calls

IDENTIFICATION

Similar in size and appearance to the Marsh Tit, but plumper, less smart and with a larger head. Black cap extends down to back and is dull, not glossy. Black bib extends onto throat and is less clean-cut. Brownish-grey upperparts are relieved by a distinctive pale wing panel. Flanks are buff. Bill is black and legs dark grey. Juvenile is similar.

LOCATION	DATE/TIME

STATUS AND HABITS

A local and decreasing resident species, thinly distributed across S Britain and extending N into S Scotland. Exclusively a woodland bird, preferring damp conditions with plenty of rotten stumps in which it excavates a nest chamber. Tolerant of conifer woods, particularly in the N of its range. Like the Marsh Tit, it frequents low, dense vegetation. The Willow Tit is less active and quieter than most tit species, making detection of this uncommon bird more difficult.

KEY FACT

The nest chamber is excavated by both sexes, and is lined with Rabbit down, woodchips and moss. Only the female incubates the 8–10 eggs, which hatch late Apr–early May.

NUTHATCH
Sitta europaea

FACT FIL

SIZE Length 14cm **HABITAT** Mixed woodland, wood pasture, parks **FOOD** Nuts, seeds, spiders, insects
VOICE Fast *chu-chu-chu* song and slow piping; loud *chwit-chwit* call

IDENTIFICATION

Distinctive plump bird, with short tail and long, stout bill. Adult upperparts are all blue-grey. Cheeks and throat are white, merging into orange-buff underparts and, in male, darker chestnut flanks. Long, narrow black eye-stripe curls down onto sides of neck. Undertail is mottled white and chestnut. Bill is black and legs yellow-brown. Juvenile is duller.

LOCATION	DATE/TIME

KEY FACT

Nuthatches are hole-nesters, usually preferring existing chambers that they can excavate further to the required size. The entrance hole is modified and reduced in size by plastering with hard mud.

STATUS AND HABITS

Common and widespread **S** species in Britain, which has extended its range **N** into Scotland over recent decades. Nuthatches are sedentary, so the current range extension is significant. They prefer large, mature trees in open woodland and parkland. They are particularly noisy and active, constantly on the move. Most commonly, Nuthatches are seen on tree trunks and large branches, where they move in jerky leaps, often head first down the trunk. They also visit garden feeders for nuts. Their flight is undulating with frequent wing closures.

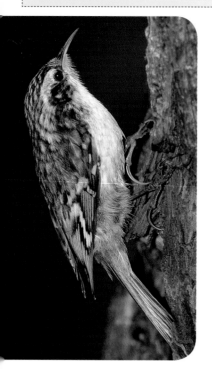

TREECREEPER
Certhia familiaris

FACT FIL

SIZE Length 12.5cm HABITAT Mature, mainly broadleaved woodland, parkland FOOD Insects, spiders, woodlice VOICE Song is a thin, high-pitched cadence; rapidly repeated *tsuu* call

IDENTIFICATION

Cryptically coloured, unobtrusive bird. Adult is predominantly brown above and white below. Upperparts are brown, heavily mottled and speckled buff and grey – vermiculated. Has a broad, curving white supercilium beneath a finely speckled crown. Close-wing pattern is complicated, with yellowish-buff angled wingbar and pale panel. Underparts are silky white. Long, thin, decurved bill is brown.

STATUS AND HABITS

A common and widespread species throughout Britain wherever there are mature woodlands. Its preferred behaviour is to cling to tree trunks, using the stiff tail as support, and to glean insects and spiders from beneath the bark. It often moves up the trunk in jerky hops, then flies down to the base of the next tree to start the process again. Treecreepers can be difficult to find, owing to their camouflage and very high-pitched call, outside the hearing range of many people.

LOCATION

DATE/TIME

KEY FACT

In winter, after foraging through mixed woodlands in loose association with tit flocks, this species roosts singly, jammed into crevices of large trees with heavily fissured bark.

JAY
Garrulus glandarius

SIZE Length 34–35cm **HABITAT** Dense broadleaved and conifer woodland, parks **FOOD** Varied vegetable matter, young birds, eggs, small mammals, insects **VOICE** Harsh, far-carrying *skaak-skaak* call

FACT FIL

IDENTIFICATION

Distinctive colourful crow. Adult body is warm pinkish brown, with rump, undertail and most of face white. Crown is finely streaked black, and has a broad black moustachial smudge. Wings are black with a prominent white patch at base of inner flight feathers and a shiny blue patch at shoulder. Bill is black and legs pale brown. Juvenile is duller.

LOCATION	DATE/TIME

STATUS AND HABITS

A resident species found throughout
England, Wales and S Scotland, but absent
from the far N. Although large and brightly
coloured, Jays can be difficult to see, as they
perch in dense foliage around the canopy
of large trees and stay still after landing.
Their raucous, shrieking call gives away
their presence. The buoyant flight, with
undulating flaps and glides on rounded
wings, is distinctive, and birds heading away
from an observer show the clear black and
white pattern of their rump and tail.

KEY FACT
Jays are infrequent
garden visitors, but can be seen on large
lawns in winter, when their bouncy,
hopping gait is distinctive. Such
individuals will be burying acorns
for a sustained winter food supply.

MAGPIE
Pica pica

FACT FILE

SIZE Length 44–46cm **HABITAT** Open country, farmland, hedgerows, habitation **FOOD** Insects, small mammals, birds and eggs, varied vegetable matter **VOICE** Rapid, chattering *chacker-chacker-chacker*

IDENTIFICATION

Distinctive and unmistakable black and white crow with a long, graduated black tail. Shoulders and belly are bright, clean white, contrasting with rest of plumage, which is glossy black with purple, bluish and green sheens. In flight, wing feathers show a broad patch of white at base. Bill and legs are black. Juvenile is duller, with a shorter tail.

LOCATION	DATE/TIME

KEY FACT

Although the Magpie has long been suspected by the public as a cause of songbird declines because of its liking for eggs and nestlings, recent work has shown that the species does not have an effect on the population levels of small birds.

STATUS AND HABITS

A locally abundant resident in **S** Britain, and patchily and more thinly distributed in Scotland. It is traditionally a bird of open, lightly wooded habitats, but where common has spread into suburban and urban situations. Small numbers are often seen together, giving rise to the nursery rhyme 'One for Sorrow'. It is conspicuous where present, perching on wires and flying slowly with characteristic weak flutters and glides, and 'chacking' conversationally. It an obvious roadside bird, commonly feeding on roadkills.

JACKDAW
Corvus monedula

SIZE Length 33–34cm **HABITAT** Sea cliffs, mountains, mature trees, human habitation **FOOD** Mainly insects, earthworms, small birds and mammals, plus cereals, seeds, fruit and berries **VOICE** Loud *kjack*

IDENTIFICATION

Smallish crow, appearing all black at a distance. Close views reveal a glossy black crown with a purplish sheen, and glossy black wings and tail with a bluish sheen. Face and nape are velvety grey, merging into underparts, which are entirely dull, dark grey. Adult has a distinctive whitish eye. Bill is short and black, and legs black. Juvenile is duller with a brown eye.

KEY FACT

Jackdaws are more dainty than other crows, walking with a quick, jaunty action on the ground. They are also noticeably acrobatic in the air, particularly when gathered in large social groups.

LOCATION	DATE/TIME

STATUS AND HABITS

A common and widespread resident bird, occurring throughout the
British Isles except the extreme **NW** of Scotland. It prefers lightly
wooded areas, particularly parkland with plenty of mature trees and old
timber. It is a hole-nester, though will use the bases of massive old stick
nests of other species. It is loosely social, with pairs nesting close together.
In the treeless **N** it breeds on sea cliffs, while in towns and villages it
makes its home in church towers and unused chimneys.

RAVEN
Corvus corax

SIZE Length 64cm; wingspan 130–150cm
HABITAT Open country, coasts, mountains, marginal farmland
FOOD Carrion, mammals, birds, some insects and seeds
VOICE Deep, repeated, honking *prruk-prruk* flight call

IDENTIFICATION

Our largest crow, the size of a Buzzard, with long wings and a long, wedge-shaped tail. All black with a purplish and brownish sheen to wings and tail. Has shaggy throat feathers and a massive, deep bill with a curved tip. Legs and strong-clawed feet are black. In flight, long wings are markedly fingered. First clue to identification is often the loud, tonal, honking call.

LOCATION	DATE/TIME

KEY FACT

The Raven is currently spreading rapidly E across Britain, occupying increasingly lowland and less remote habitats. In these areas it finds nest sites on bridges and pylons, in addition to tall, mature trees.

STATUS AND HABITS

Mainly a bird of W Britain, occurring from the S to the extreme N. Traditionally a bird of high, remote mountains and coasts, the Raven now also occupies open lowland habitats. It is an accomplished flyer, using windy locations and updraughts to great advantage. In late winter, breeding displays involve spectacular acrobatic flights, including upside-down twists, accompanied by the evocative call. It is a very early nesting species, laying its eggs in Feb.

CARRION CROW
Corvus corone

FACT FIL

SIZE Length 45–47cm **HABITAT** Farmland, upland and lowland open country with scattered trees **FOOD** Varied: carrion, mammals, birds, insects and worms, seeds and fruit **VOICE** Repeated *kawr* call

IDENTIFICATION
Classic crow with all-black plumage, bill and legs. Fresh adult feathers are faintly glossed green and lilac. Has a stout bill with a curved tip and well-feathered base; this feature distinguishes it from the similar Rook, particularly when juvenile. Smaller size, rounded tail and lack of shaggy throat distinguish it from the Raven.

LOCATION	DATE/TIME

STATUS AND HABITS

A common and widespread species across most of Britain, though in Scotland it occurs only S and E of a line between Aberdeen and the Clyde, giving way to the Hooded Crow in the N and W. Usually a more solitary species than the Rook, though large flocks can occur at communal roosts, birds flying in during the evening from a wide catchment. A regular carrion feeder, this crow is commonly seen along roadsides eating roadkill Rabbits and Pheasants. Its flight is listless, with shallow wingbeats.

KEY FACT
Until recently, Carrion and Hooded crows were considered to be the same species, separated only by geographical location. Modern studies have elevated them to separate species status.

HOODED CROW
Corvus cornix

SIZE Length 45–47cm **HABITAT** Open country, farmland, uplands, coasts **FOOD** Very varied: birds and eggs, small mammals, invertebrates, vegetable matter **VOICE** Repeated *cawr-cawr-cawr*

IDENTIFICATION

Same size as the Carrion Crow, but much of its body plumage is pale grey instead of black. Has a grey mantle, back, rump, shoulders, and underparts from lower breast to undertail. Head, throat, wings and tail are black. Bill and legs are black. Juvenile is similar to adult but grey areas are buffish. In flight, pale grey of underparts extends into 'armpits'.

LOCATION	DATE/TIME

STATUS AND HABITS

The N and W equivalent of the Carrion Crow, and an abundant breeding resident in W Scotland and the Isle of Man. In winter, occasional wandering birds turn up in England. It is bird of open country, preferring grazing land in the lowlands, and is common across hills and mountains in uplands. In winter, it is particularly fond of coasts, where it forages along the tideline. It is a catholic feeder, commonly taking small birds and their eggs, and eating molluscs on the coast.

KEY FACT In Europe, the Hooded Crow replaces the Carrion Crow in the E and N of the Continent, extending into Asia. There is a small area of overlap through E Europe.

ROOK
Corvus frugilegus

FACT FIL

SIZE Length 44–46cm **HABITAT** Agricultural land with adjacent tall, mature trees **FOOD** Cereals, roots, insects, earthworms, some carrion **VOICE** *Kaah* call, varying in pitch

IDENTIFICATION

Adult is all black except for whitish bare area of skin around base of bill and face. Steep forehead and round head combine with narrower pale bill to distinguish this crow. Black plumage is glossy with a greenish and purplish sheen. In flight, shows deeply fingered wings and a rounded tail. Legs are black with shaggy thigh feathers. Juvenile lacks bare facial skin.

LOCATION	DATE/TIME

STATUS AND HABITS

A common resident throughout Britain, found wherever open country contains mature trees, though avoiding dense woodland. Gregarious at all times, the Rook is famously a colonial breeder and is found in large flocks through the rest of the year. This species nests early in the year, adults returning to traditional colonies during winter to repair nests and cement pair bonds with noisy calling and display. Village churchyards with tall trees commonly hold a rookery. Flocks forage in fields, feeding mainly on invertebrates.

KEY FACT

Rooks commonly used to select the English Elm for traditional nesting colonies. Since the disappearance of this tree through Dutch elm disease, however, they have had to find alternative nesting sites, often in smaller roadside trees.

STARLING
Sturnus vulgaris

SIZE **Length 21.5cm** HABITAT **Wide variety of open**
country and urban habitats FOOD **Varied invertebrates and**
vegetable matter VOICE **Song is a lively medley incorporating**
mimicry; *tcheerr* **call**

FACT FIL

IDENTIFICATION

Medium-sized bird, with triangular wings in flight and a compact shape.
Adult has glossy black plumage with buff spotting, and fine buff streaks
on head. Has brownish wings and a greenish gloss on back, and is purplish
below. In summer, bill is yellow and legs pink. In winter, bill is black. Juvenile
looks like a different species, with pale brownish-grey plumage, a black bill,
and a black line extending to eye.

SPOTTER'S CHART

LOCATION	DATE/TIME

KEY FACT
In autumn and winter, very large flocks of Starlings gather together for communal roosting. Before settling for the night, these flocks undertake spectacular flying displays, visible against the setting sun.

STATUS AND HABITS

A common resident and partial migrant throughout Britain, with some birds moving S in winter, to be replaced by birds from the Continent. A gregarious nature and tolerance of humans make this a very conspicuous bird. It is common in our towns and cities, using buildings for nesting in holes and crevices. In the countryside, it is common around farm buildings, traditionally selecting natural nest-holes in mature trees. Starlings have a varied song, often mimicking other species and artificial sounds.

HOUSE SPARROW
Passer domesticus

FACT FILE

SIZE Length 14–15cm **HABITAT** Human habitation, cities, towns, villages **FOOD** Seeds, insects, buds, fruit **VOICE** *Cheep* and *chirrp* calls, strung together in simple song

IDENTIFICATION

Adult male is warm brown above, grey below. Has a grey crown, black eye-stripe, black bib with broken lower margin across breast, and dull white cheeks. Bill is black. Has a grey rump, dark tail and white wingbar. Female is uniform grey-brown above, dingy white below. Has a pale buff supercilium and pale wing-feather edging. Bill is grey. Juvenile resembles female. All have pink legs.

MALE

LOCATION	DATE/TIME

STATUS AND HABITS

Widely distributed across the British Isles, though populations have declined markedly in recent decades. A sedentary, resident species, favouring habitats in close proximity to humans. House Sparrows breed in loose colonies around houses and other buildings, often siting their nests under eaves or in disused chimneys. Their conversational cheeping has been a common accompaniment to our suburban gardens. Males displaying in the spring puff out their chest, cock their tail and flutter drooping wings, calling loudly and repeatedly.

KEY FACT

The decline in House Sparrow populations is still a bit of a mystery. It is thought that the reduced availability of insect food due to modern agricultural practices, combined with urban pollution, may be contributing to their demise.

MALE

TREE SPARROW
Passer montanus

FACT FILE

SIZE Length 14cm **HABITAT** Lightly wooded areas, hedgerows, orchards, gardens, farms **FOOD** Seeds, insects **VOICE** Musical, high-pitched *chee-ip*

IDENTIFICATION

Neater, brighter version of the House Sparrow, with the sexes alike. Adult has a rich chestnut crown and nape, and white cheeks with an isolated black patch. White extends around neck in a collar. Black extends from bill to eye and to a neat black bib. Upperparts are bright brown, underparts whitish. Has two creamy-white wingbars. Bill is black and legs pale brown. Juvenile is similar but duller.

LOCATION	DATE/TIME

KEY FACT

The Tree Sparrow population has fluctuated markedly over the last century, with a large increase 50 years ago. In recent decades the species' fortunes have reversed, with a decline to only a tenth of its previous numbers.

STATUS AND HABITS

Quite widely, but locally distributed across Britain, and less likely to be encountered in the far W and N. A resident species and semi-colonial breeder, nesting in tree-holes, crevices behind vegetation on buildings and, increasingly, in nestboxes – such schemes have success in attracting and growing colonies of this declining species. Both sexes share the incubation of eggs. In winter, Tree Sparrows join mixed flocks of finches and buntings to forage for seeds across stubble and winter crops.

GOLDFINCH
Carduelis carduelis

SIZE Length 12cm **HABITAT** Gardens, parks, weedy
fields, brownfield sites, scrub **FOOD** Seeds, occasionally small
insects **VOICE** Bright, sweet, tinkling song; liquid *tswitt-witti-witt* call

FACT FILE

IDENTIFICATION

Small finch, unmistakable in adult plumage with a bright yellow panel on
black wing, a bright red face around bill, and broad, vertical black and
white bands on head. Body is overall buffish pink, whiter underneath and
with a black tail. Has white spots to tips of tail and flight feathers. Juvenile
is greyer than adult and mottled, with a reduced yellow wing panel and
plain head.

LOCATION	DATE/TIME

KEY FACT Goldfinches are now commonly seen at garden bird tables, especially where their favoured Nyjer seeds are provided in specially designed feeders. Their narrow bill is an expert tool for getting hold of the fine seeds.

STATUS AND HABITS

Feeds on seeds extracted directly from plants, perching acrobatically amongst flower heads. Flits from plant to plant, appearing to flutter butterfly-like just above the ground. A gregarious species, gathering in small flocks that fly with noticeable but light, dance-like undulations and twitter conversationally to each other. Often seen perched on the highest and outermost branches of Common Alders and birches, from where its cheerful song is delivered in spring. In autumn, the large seedheads of Wild Teasel are a favoured food source, with these small finches perching easily amongst the spikes.

CHAFFINCH
Fringilla coelebs

FACT FILE

SIZE Length 14.5cm HABITAT Woodland, farmland, parks, gardens FOOD Seeds, fruit, insects VOICE Song is a loud, musical rattle, ending with a flourish; *chwink* and *wheet* calls

IDENTIFICATION

Adult male is distinctive and colourful, with a pink face, breast and belly, blue-grey crown and nape, chestnut-brown back and greenish rump. Has dark wings with two white wingbars, and a longish, dark, cleft tail with prominent white outer feathers. Bill is slate blue in summer, otherwise dull pinkish grey. Legs are pale brown. Female is duller olive-brown above, greyish below. Juvenile resembles female.

MALE

LOCATION	DATE/TIME

STATUS AND HABITS

FEMALE

One of our commonest and most widespread birds, the Chaffinch is a resident species, breeding throughout the British Isles, including the islands around the **N** of Scotland. It is a bird both of woodland and open country, and chooses a wide variety of vegetation in which to nest, particularly small trees, hedgerows and large gardens. The breeding male is a familiar songster, even in towns and cities where there are trees. He is brightly coloured, whilst the female is more cryptic.

KEY FACT

Chaffinches are common members of mixed flocks of feeding finches in winter, ranging over stubble and weedy fields. When taking flight, their white shoulder patch, wingbar and outer-tail feathers are conspicuous.

BRAMBLING
Fringilla montifringilla

FACT FILE

SIZE Length 14cm **HABITAT** Beech woods, stubble fields, parks, large gardens **FOOD** Seeds (particularly Beech-mast), berries **VOICE** Hoarse *chucc-chucc-chucc* flight call; male has a trumpet-like *dwee* call

IDENTIFICATION

In flight, note its distinctive black and orange plumage and white rump. Adult summer male has a glossy black head and mantle, mottled brown in winter. Has a dark tail and wings with two white-edged, pale orange-buff wingbars, a warm orange breast and shoulder patch, and a white belly and undertail. Bill is yellowish with a black tip and legs flesh-brown. Female and juvenile are duller.

WINTER MALE

LOCATION	DATE/TIME

STATUS AND HABITS

A widespread winter visitor and passage migrant, numbers varying according to the food supply, particularly Beech-mast. A very few pairs have bred in N Scotland. Its preferred natural habitat in winter is open Beech woodland, where flocks are found feeding on the seeds underneath large, spreading trees. In flight, its white rump is a prominent identification feature. Bramblings are also common members of mixed-species winter finch flocks, feeding on farmland and favouring stubble fields and yards with spilt grain.

WINTER FEMALE

KEY FACT

Now that the quality and diversity of commercial bird food is so high, Bramblings are increasingly visiting garden feeders. The species often starts joining its fellow finches in the garden during the coldest spells of winter.

GREENFINCH
Carduelis chloris

FACT FILE

SIZE Length 15cm **HABITAT** Open country with trees, parks, gardens, orchards, farmland in winter **FOOD** Seeds, fruit and berries, insects **VOICE** Song is a warbling twitter; long nasal *tsweee* call

IDENTIFICATION

Distinguished by its pale, stout bill, olive-green plumage with a bright yellow-green rump, and bright yellow wing patches and sides to tail. Adult male is bright and clean. Female is duller. Juvenile is browner above, paler below and with noticeable fine, dark brown streaking. Legs are pinkish flesh. In flight, the species' dumpy form and cleft tail are good identification features.

MALE

LOCATION	DATE/TIME

STATUS AND HABITS

Found throughout the British Isles as a very common resident species. Greenfinches avoid dense woodland, preferring open habitats with plenty of mature trees. In the N uplands they will live in moorland conifer plantations. They are one of our most frequent garden visitors, and regularly nest in mature gardens with shrubberies and hedgerows, where they feed their chicks on insects and other invertebrates. In winter, they join other finches to feed on farmland stubble.

FEMALE

KEY FACT

In spring and summer, adult male Greenfinches undertake interesting song flights from the tops of tall trees. They circle around with exaggerated slow and lazy wingbeats, these often asymmetrical, while making their wheezy calls.

SISKIN
Carduelis spinus

SIZE **Length** 12cm **HABITAT** Coniferous woodland, riverine Common Alders and birches, gardens **FOOD** Tree seeds, buds and berries **VOICE** Song is a sweet, wheezy twitter; piping *tsuu* call **FACT FILE**

IDENTIFICATION

Small, neat finch with a deeply cleft tail. Adults have blackish wings with a yellow-green wingbar and yellow flash on flight feathers. Adult male is green above and yellow below, with a black crown and chin. Black tail is edged with bright yellow flashes. Belly and undertail are whitish, streaked black. Has a sharp, pale bill and brown legs. Female lacks black crown. Juvenile is browner and more streaked.

MALE

LOCATION	DATE/TIME

STATUS AND HABITS

An increasingly widespread resident,
commonest in the **N** where there is plenty
of coniferous forest and birch woodland.
This finch uses its narrow, sharply pointed bill
to great effect in extracting the seeds from
spruce cones and other tree species. In autumn
and winter, small flocks gather together and
are seen at migration watchpoints as birds
interchange with the **Continental European**
population. In recent decades the Siskin has
become a common garden visitor, usually
feeding on peanuts.

KEY FACT Siskins keep to the tops
of tall conifers, and are delicately acrobatic
in their efforts to reach ripe seeds. They
fly high with a quick, light action and their
piping call is the best clue to their presence.

JUVENILE

BULLFINCH
Pyrrhula pyrrhula

SIZE Length 15cm **HABITAT** Woodland edges, hedgerows, gardens **FOOD** Buds, seeds, berries, insects in summer **VOICE** Gentle, rich, piping *teu* call

FACT FILE

MALE

IDENTIFICATION
Dumpy, plump finch with a stubby black bill. Male has a glossy black cap, blue-grey nape and mantle, and black wings and tail with a broad dove-grey wingbar. Conspicuous white rump is obvious in flight. Cheeks and underparts are bright pinkish red, with a white undertail. Legs are pinkish. Female shares male's pattern but red is replaced by pinkish buff. Juvenile resembles female but lacks black cap.

KEY FACT
The Bullfinch's soft, piping call is surprisingly far-carrying, and the presence of these shy birds can be confirmed as they fly with a weakish, dancing flight along hedgerows displaying their conspicuous white rump.

LOCATION	DATE/TIME

STATUS AND HABITS

A resident species that is less likely to undertake significant seasonal movements than other finches. Fairly widespread throughout Britain, but its range is shrinking and its population decreasing. A shy and unobtrusive species, preferring dense, scrubby vegetation adjacent to sources of buds, particularly orchards, and fruit bushes in gardens. More often heard than seen, as its low, piping call is often repeated from within cover. Not generally found in flocks with other finch species; pairs and families stay together throughout the year.

FEMALE

HAWFINCH
Coccothraustes coccothraustes

FACT FIL

SIZE Length 18cm **HABITAT** Mature, open deciduous woodland **FOOD** Seed kernels, Beech-mast, insects in summer **VOICE** Loud *tic* call, often given in flight

IDENTIFICATION
Bulky finch, whose massive bill and large head give it a top-heavy appearance. Adult male is predominantly orange-buff with dark wings, a grey nape and a large white shoulder patch. Has black around eye, base of bill and on chin. Short, dark tail has a white patch across tip, broadest in centre. Bill is horn-coloured and legs pinkish. Female is duller. Juvenile is brown with mottled underparts.

MALE

LOCATION	DATE/TIME

> **KEY FACT**
>
> The Hawfinch's massive seed-cracking bill enables it to open cherry stones, and it is the only British bird that can successfully tackle the seeds of Hornbeam, a favoured woodland tree.

STATUS AND HABITS

Prefers mature open woodlands with large broadleaved trees. Fairly widely distributed across England and Wales, and N to central Scotland, but local and scarce. Its shy and retiring nature, and its habit of staying in the dense canopy cover of tall trees, makes this species difficult to see. It is more often encountered in winter, when small numbers feed on Beech-mast and other seeds on the woodland floor. Even then, it can disappear surprisingly easily and quietly when disturbed.

FEMALE

LESSER REDPOLL
Carduelis cabaret

FACT FILE

SIZE Length 13–14cm **HABITAT** Conifer plantations, Common Alder and birch woodland **FOOD** Seeds, insects **VOICE** Trilling, chattering song; fast *chuchuchuhuh* call

IDENTIFICATION

Small, heavily streaked brownish finch with a longish, deeply forked tail. Adult male has a red forecrown, black chin and whitish supercilium. Has two prominent white wingbars and a pinkish breast. Bill is yellow and legs black. Adult female is similar, but has less red on crown and lacks pink breast. Both sexes have a streaked, pale silvery belly. Juvenile lacks red crown.

MALE

LOCATION	DATE/TIME

STATUS AND HABITS

A common and widely distributed resident wherever there are coniferous trees and seed-bearing Common Alders and birches, particularly along rivers. In autumn and winter, our population is swelled by immigrants from the Continent. The Lesser Redpoll is another finch of the high treetops, acrobatic in its search for seeds at the tips of slender branches, and can be difficult to see well. In winter, it forms flocks and stays in woodland, though some birds are starting to visit garden feeders where their preferred seeds are provided.

MALE

KEY FACT
Lesser Redpoll is one of a number of redpoll species occurring in the British Isles, all of which are similar in looks and habits. This species is our commonest.

LINNET
Carduelis cannabina

SIZE Length 13.5cm **HABITAT** Heaths, commons, hedgerows, farmland, saltmarshes **FOOD** Seeds, insects, spiders **VOICE** Song is a soft, musical twittering; conversational *tihtihtihtit* flight call

IDENTIFICATION

Adult male is prettily coloured. Has a grey head with a red forecrown, chestnut mantle and wing coverts, blackish flight feathers and white-edged tail. Chin is white and breast washed crimson. Rest of underparts are greyish white, streaked pink on flanks. Bill is grey and legs dark brown. Female lacks red, and has black-streaked brown upperparts and brown-streaked buff underparts. Juvenile is uniform brown, heavily streaked darker.

MALE

LOCATION	DATE/TIME

KEY FACT Flocks of Linnets flit over winter farmland in waves. Their flight is rapid and undulating, with the whole flock appearing to waver and dance above the fields. On the ground they are inconspicuous.

JUVENILE

STATUS AND HABITS

Common and widespread resident throughout the British Isles, breeding as far N as the Shetland Isles. Linnets prefer scrubby, open habitats, particularly heaths with gorse, young conifer plantations in uplands and rough farmland. In the breeding season, the male will perch prominently amongst the yellow gorse flowers, singing a pleasant jumble of twittering notes, and when seen well is a striking bird. In winter, this species forms large flocks that vacate the breeding habitats and range over seedy stubble fields on farmland.

CORN BUNTING
Emberiza calandra

SIZE **Length** 18cm **HABITAT** Farmland with hedgerows **FOOD** Seeds, buds and berries, insects and other invertebrates **VOICE** Song is an accelerated ticking, ending in a jangling flourish; *quit-it-it* call

FACT FILE

IDENTIFICATION

Large, bulky, rather uniform brown bunting. Upperparts are buff-brown, heavily streaked darker. Underparts are whitish, with a gorget of finer black streaks across upper breast. Large, conical bill is pinkish, and large, beady eye black. Has a pale-edged, dark brown wingbar. Longish tail is blackish brown. Flight action includes fluttering wings and dangling legs. Rather ungainly bird.

LOCATION	DATE/TIME

STATUS AND HABITS

An uncommon, local resident species whose population is declining and whose range is contracting. Current strongholds are chalky farmland in **SE England** and agricultural systems of the far **W**, from **Cornwall** to **N Scotland**. Prefers open country away from trees, particularly arable fields and large expanses of grassland, with food-bearing boundaries such as hedges and stone walls in uplands. In the breeding season, the male's song, though tuneless, is distinctive, with the jangling flourish described as sounding like a bunch of keys.

KEY FACT

Modern intensive agriculture has caused the decline of the Corn Bunting across Britain. Agri-environment incentives are now available to encourage farmers to manage field edges and hedgerows to provide more food and better nesting sites.

YELLOWHAMMER
Emberiza citrinella

SIZE Length 16.5cm **HABITAT** Grassland, arable land with hedgerows, heaths, stubble fields in winter **FOOD** Seeds, corn, fruit, insects **VOICE** Song is described as a 'little-bit-of-bread-and-no-cheese'; ringing *twink* call

FACT FILE

IDENTIFICATION

Adult summer male has bright lemon yellow on head and underparts, a chestnut mantle, shoulders and rump, blackish-brown wings, and a dark tail with prominent white outer feathers. Has black smudges behind the eye and on cheeks, and a chestnut suffusion of streaks on the breast and flanks. Bill is grey and legs pink. The adult winter male has subdued colouring. The female is duller with stronger facial streaks. Juvenile is much more streaked.

MALE

LOCATION	DATE/TIME

KEY FACT

Like many buntings, Yellowhammers feed almost exclusively on the ground, where their hopping gait and habit of constantly flicking white outer-tail feathers sideways draws attention.

STATUS AND HABITS

A generally well-distributed resident, occurring throughout the British Isles except for some island groups and parts of N Scotland. The population is thinning out across the range, however, as intensive agriculture fails to provide enough food and cover. Where it does occur in summer, the Yellowhammer is a conspicuous bird, the male attracting attention with its distinctive and famous thin, wheezy song. In winter, birds move from scrubby habitats and are found almost entirely in mixed finch flocks on arable stubble fields.

FEMALE

CIRL BUNTING
Emberiza cirlus

FACT FILE

SIZE Length 16cm HABITAT Pasture, hedgerows, bushy slopes, often near the sea FOOD Corn and weed seeds, insects VOICE Song is a rattling repetition of the same note; thin *zit* call

IDENTIFICATION

Olive-yellow and brown bunting. Adult male has a striking head pattern with a black line through eye and on chin, fine black streaks on crown and a yellow face. Underparts are yellow with a greenish and chestnut breast-band. Upperparts are chestnut, rump olive-green. Tail is dark with white outer feathers. Bill is grey and legs pink. Female lacks male's head pattern and is duller. Juvenile is buff-brown, heavily streaked.

MALE

SPOTTER'S CHART

LOCATION	DATE/TIME

STATUS AND HABITS

Now restricted to a very few locations in the **SW** of England where habitats have been specially managed to encourage the breeding and winter survival of this sedentary resident. Can be unobtrusive and difficult to detect other than in early spring, when the male sings conspicuously from a hedgerow tree. The song, a rather tuneless rattle on one note, is reminiscent of that of the Lesser Whitethroat. In winter, small flocks gather on weedy stubble fields, especially above coastal sea cliffs near breeding sites.

MALE

KEY FACT

Cirl Buntings were previously much more widespread across the chalk farmland of S England. Their continuing survival as a British species is dependent on careful and precise management of their summer and winter habitats.

INDEX

PHOTOGRAPHIC ACKNOWLEDGEMENTS

Photographs supplied by Nature Photographers Ltd. All photographs by Paul Sterry except for the those on the following pages:

Frank Blackburn: 64, 141; Colin Carver: 46; Phil Green: 25; Ernie Janes: 16, 27; Owen Newman: 20; Philip Newman: 107; WS Paton: 26; Richard Revels: 51, 185; Don Smith: 55, 56; Roger Tidman: 24, 63, 79, 95, 152, 178; EK Thompson: 57.